the joy of

Brewing Cider,
Mead, and Herbal Wine

How to Craft Seasonal Fast-Brew Favorites at Home

Nancy Koziol

Skyhorse Publishing

Skyhorse Publishing books may be purchased in bulk at special
discounts for sales promotion, corporate gifts, fund-raising,
or educational purposes. Special editions can also be created to
specifications. For details, contact the Special Sales Department,
Skyhorse Publishing, 307 West 36th Street, 11th Floor, New York,
NY 10018 or info@skyhorsepublishing.com.

Skyhorse® and Skyhorse Publishing® are registered trademarks of
Skyhorse Publishing, Inc.®, a Delaware corporation.

Visit our website at www.skyhorsepublishing.com.

10 9 8 7 6 5

Library of Congress Cataloging-in-Publication Data is available on file.

Cover image courtesy of istockphoto.com

Print ISBN: 978-1-5107-3494-4
Ebook ISBN: 978-1-5107-3495-1

Printed in China

CONTENTS

1. Welcome to Home Brewing

IF YOU'VE BEEN thinking about home brewing but want something quicker, easier, and more cost effective than home brewing beer or making wine at home, you've come to the right place. This book will teach you how to brew mead, hard cider, and herbal wine using the quickest, most minimalist methods possible.

From the fewest steps to the least amount of equipment and ingredients, you'll not only learn how to brew but also pick up some good trivia about the history of these beverages. Finally, this book explores the sustainable, eco-friendly side of brewing, including tips for vegans. If you're a beginner, I recommend reading through the first few chapters on tools and processes before diving into the recipes. Cheers!

Why Brew One-Gallon Batches?

Every recipe in this book is for one gallon of either mead, cider, or herbal wine. Why is that? It's all about keeping it ethical. One-gallon batches make it easy to live a conscious lifestyle while enjoying home-brewed alcohol.

Home brewing is not easy. It sounds easy. It looks easy. But it's not easy. Especially in the beginning. In my own brewing experience I have lost several batches thanks to oxygenation, temperature issues within my home, and yeast that just didn't want to behave. This got me thinking, early in my journey, about waste. Using mead as an example, a one-gallon batch uses two to three pounds of honey plus a significant amount of water to clean and sterilize the equipment. Even with the water-saving offsets I employ in my brewing, there is still waste. By keeping the batches small, we minimize waste when a batch doesn't go the way we planned. Once you're more experienced and your batches are consistently turning out well, then maybe it's time to move on to larger batches.

Another reason for one-gallon batches has to do with moderation. It's great to enjoy wine, beer, mead, cider, and cocktails. It's especially great to enjoy ones that you made yourself. But brewing large batches means having more alcohol in the house. Just like you'll drink more water in a day if it's readily available, you're more likely to drink more alcohol if you have it in the house, especially if you're worried about it getting stale or flattening. One-gallon batches allow you to pace yourself and pour a glass to enjoy rather than drink to avoid waste.

On that note, if you ever feel that your drinking is becoming problematic, please reach out:

In the US (English or Spanish) call 1.800.662.4357 - 24/7, 365
    days a year
In Canada call the Canadian Centre on Substance Use and
    Addiction
In the UK call 0300 123 1110
In Australia call 1800 131 350

2. Home Brewing Equipment

BEFORE YOU START brewing, it's important to have the right equipment. Here are the absolute must-have basics, plus a few things that will make your life so much easier.

Equipment for Preparation

Every home brewer starts a brew day by cleaning and sanitizing, but regular detergent and soap won't do.

Detergent

The first step in your prep is cleaning. Powdered Brewing Wash (PBW) is a favorite of home brewers. It gets the job done without

the need for scrubbing, and is hard on dirt and grime, but easy on skin. For deep cleaning, soak equipment overnight and then rinse in the morning before brewing. For regular cleaning, just follow the directions on the container and get ready to brew. It only takes about thirty minutes. PBW can handle the toughest stains and is perfect for cleaning up the carboy used in primary fermentation, which often has caked-on yeast.

There are one-step cleaners on the market that both clean and sanitize. These are great for caps, stoppers, airlocks, thermometers, and other pieces of your brewing kit that don't get lots of organic material stuck on them. But for carboys—especially those used in primary fermentation—one-step cleaners just don't work as well.

Sanitizer

The second step in your prep is sanitizing. After cleaning to get rid of any organic materials, sanitizing removes everything else and prevents bacteria from infecting your brew.

Star San works well and can be found at your local home brewing shop or online.

Brewing, Fermenting, Racking, and Bottling Equipment

The process of brewing includes several stages that use various pieces of equipment for heating, mixing, transferring, and bottling.

Two One-Gallon Carboys

These jugs, also called demijohns, are used during primary and secondary fermentation. You need two to start. They come in plastic or glass, but go for the glass option. Glass is more sustainable and plastic can develop scratches, the perfect place for bacteria to hang out.

Also, plastic is terrible for the environment and low quality plastic is bad for your health. A glass carboy leaves far less of a footprint, lasts longer, and is easier to keep clean and sanitized.

Carboys can be found at homebrew shops, some hardware stores, and online.

Two Drilled Stoppers

You only need one while you're brewing, but get a backup. Also called a bung, this rubber stopper fits the top of your carboy, but with room for the air-lock. Make sure that the stopper fits a one-gallon carboy.

Airlock

This small plastic device fits into a drilled stopper. Place a little water in it (there's a fill line) and watch it go. Your airlock tells you fermentation is happening by bubbling happily as the yeast releases CO_2. It is used during primary and secondary fermentation.

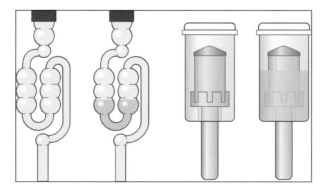

There are two types of airlocks used in home brewing. The three-piece airlock is cylindrical and the best choice because it's easy to clean. The S-bubble airlock is great for picture-taking—it looks really cool—but is more difficult to clean and sanitize because of the many chambers.

Large Stainless Steel Pot

While you won't need to boil like in beer brewing, you will have to heat ingredients when making mead and herbal wine. A stainless steel pot is perfect and should hold at least four quarts.

Funnel

Carboy tops are small. A funnel allows you to get all of your ingredients in a carboy without any waste. When using fruit, herbs, nuts, or honey, add those first. Follow with your warm water. This leaves the funnel cleaner and also uses the water to get the most of your ingredients in your must.

Immersion Thermometer

Yeast is finicky stuff, especially when it comes to temperature. Always use a cooking thermometer so that you can pitch (add) your yeast at the right temperature.

Fermometer

Get some adhesive thermometers to pop on the outside of your glass carboys. This will help you track where you're storing your brews to make sure that you keep them at a stable temperature that is perfect for your yeast.

Rubber Tubing

Your brew will get transferred between fermentation vessels to keep it off the dead yeast. You'll do this by siphoning (see chapter 3, page 13) with rubber tubing. Get a thinner-diameter tube for easier siphoning; it takes longer to siphon with a thinner tube but it is much easier to get started.

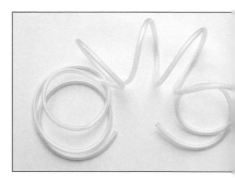

There are auto siphons (also called racking canes) on the market, which can make siphoning easier, but they take a while to get the hang of. If you choose to go that route, make sure the one you buy fits a one-gallon carboy.

Bottles

You can reuse beer bottles or use swing-top bottles—just make sure that they are safe for carbonating if you plan on carbonating your brews.

Bottle Caps

You can reuse beer bottles from your favorite brews, but you can't reuse the caps. They won't fit and seal properly. Caps are cheap and

can be bought in large quantities, and some have great designs that make them really fun.

Bottle Capper

You can't top your bottles without a bottle capper. These are easy to get the hang of and can be found at your local homebrew shop or online.

Bottling Wand

These wands make an easy time out of bottling your brew. Just press the wand to the bottom of the bottle and it will fill. Lift the wand and the flow of liquid stops. Pop on the cap and move on to the next bottle. So easy.

A Note on Materials

Always buy brewing equipment made of glass or stainless steel. These items are eco-friendly and don't wear. They also don't get scuffed as much as plastic, which means your chance for infection is far lower.

Spray Bottles and Other Sanitation Tricks

Sanitation is key to the home brewing process. It helps eliminate lingering odors and provides a pristine base for your brews. Throughout this book sanitation is discussed, but this section serves to provide some great tips for sanitizing that you may not have thought of.

1. *Invest in a spray bottle.* I prefer one with an adjustable nozzle, but any spray bottle will do. The next time you make sanitizer, scale down the measurements and make enough to fill the bottle. Keep this with you on brew days and you'll revolutionize your process.

2. *Clean first, then sanitize.* Cleaning and sanitizing are
    equally important. Each step has a different purpose
    and they work together to provide a clean brewing
    environment.

3. *Treat your work surfaces, all of them, with the same attention
    as your brewing equipment.* Use cleaner, rinse, and then
    sanitize. How? With a fine mist from that spray bottle.

4. *Get rid of that towel.* I hate wet surfaces. When I first
    started brewing I put a towel on the counter. I set my
    equipment on it as I pulled the pieces from soaking in
    the sink. Luckily I live with an experienced brewer who
    pointed out the error in my ways: towels are not sanitary.

5. *Do not trust the sanitize setting on your dishwasher.* Don't be
    tempted to load your equipment into the dishwasher and
    run it with detergent on the sanitize setting. When home
    brewers refer to sanitizing they mean using a specific acid
    solution.

6. *If it touches something that hasn't been sanitized, sanitize it.*
    Did you drop your funnel on the floor? If that happens
    in my house a dog or two are instantly over to inspect it.
    Sanitize it! Did your siphoning tube touch the floor while
    you were checking its length? Sanitize it! Are you not
    sure if you touched your spoon with unwashed hands?
    SANITIZE IT!

7. *Don't rinse!* The hardest
    thing to get used to
    when sanitizing is
    the lack of rinsing.
    You will be able to see
    remnants of sanitizer,
    and having read the
    bottle you'll not want
    it anywhere near

your brew, but rinsing it defeats the purpose. I place my
sanitized carboy upside down in a clean, sanitized pitcher
and allow it to drip until all the foam is off.

8. *Be careful.* Sanitizer is nasty stuff. Take care to keep
    it away from mucus membranes and to limit contact
    with your skin. The only things you should rinse when
    sanitizing, in fact, are your hands. Do not use sanitizer
    anywhere near food because it is poisonous. Keep
    children and animals away from sanitizer. Finally, always
    clean with a chlorine-free detergent (I recommend
    PBW). Sanitizer cannot come into contact with cleansers
    that use chlorine. If it does, dangerous chlorine gas is
    released into your brew space.

My preferred sanitizer is Star San. It's easy to use and has a
great easy-measure and -pour cap that cuts down on how much
equipment I have to use on a brew day. Five Star Chemicals' Star
San is easy to find at homebrew shops, restaurant supply stores,
and even some hardware stores. It can also be ordered online.

Different sanitizers require slightly different processes.
Your sanitizer should include instructions to follow for home
brewing.

3. How to Siphon

ASK A HOME brewer the most difficult part of home brewing and chances are they will talk about siphoning. Siphoning is not only tricky to master, but it's also vital to the health of your brews. There are no shortcuts. Why? Science.

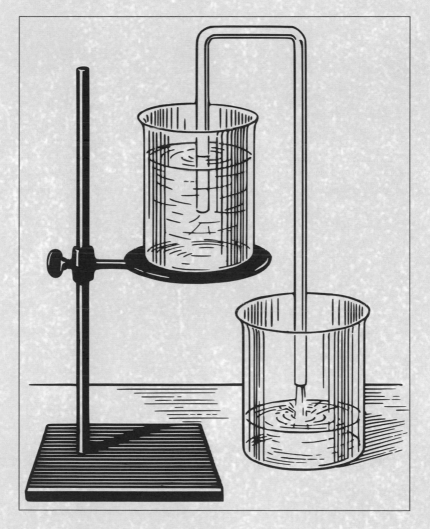

After primary fermentation, you will move your brew off of the dead yeast hanging out at the bottom of your carboy and into a second, freshly cleaned and sanitized carboy. This is done using a sanitized tube and is often called "racking." Depending on the type of brew, racking can take place more than once. Every time you rack, your brew is at risk. Prior to adding your yeast, you'll want to introduce oxygen to your must or wort through a process called aeration. Aeration can involve vigorous shaking, or you can use an oxygen tank and small tube to give the yeast plenty of oxygen. Once you've pitched your yeast, though, and fermentation has started, you'll shift to trying to avoid additional oxygen. This is because oxidation kills home brews. And oxygen helps bacteria grow. Oxygen before pitching the yeast is great. Once the yeast is pitched, oxygen is bad.

Most brews require two fermentations known as primary and secondary. This means you'll transfer your wort off of the dead yeast and other sediment into a second container where it will finish brewing and then be ready to bottle. This is the most common place where oxygen ruins the party.

If you were to pour your primary into your secondary, a few problems would arise. First, the dead yeast would travel with your mead, cider, or wine. You want to get it off the yeast so that the flavor doesn't change from the husks. Siphoning allows you to control from where you pull your brew, and you'll leave a bit above the yeast cake at the bottom so that you transfer mostly sediment-free liquid.

It's not just the yeast, though. When you pour any liquid, it splashes and develops bubbles of air. Even if you try to pour carefully down the side, you'll get some bubbles. And thus home brewing cannot be done without siphoning. Luckily, there are a few different methods. It sounds crazy, but I cannot recommend enough trying out different processes with water and two containers. Once you figure out the method that works for you, practice until you feel really confident. If I had to guess, I'd say oxygenation is the number one way homebrews get ruined, and that the oxygen is most often introduced during racking.

This book provides detailed information on two ways to siphon using only a rubber hose. YouTube is a great resource, too. Watching people do this can really help you perfect your technique.

Method #1: Using Water

One way to siphon is by using water to start the process. This is often referred to as siphoning by submersion, but a few changes have to be made in order to make the process work for home brewing.

It is important that you clean and sanitize any item used in this process, and I recommend keeping a spray bottle with sanitizer (see page 10) to help. Spraying your hands at the start of this process is not a bad idea, but don't touch your face or eat anything until after you've washed them.

You'll need:

- Spray bottle of sanitizer solution
- Rubber tubing (thinner tubing makes it easier)
- Your kitchen sink
- Your primary fermentation vessel
- Your secondary fermentation vessel, cleaned and sanitized
- A bowl to catch water
- A way to place your containers at two different heights

How to Do It:

1. Place your primary higher than your secondary. If you have a bar, put it up there and place your secondary in the sink or on the floor. If you are not able to put your secondary in the sink, place the bowl next to it.
2. Make sure the hose is cleaned and sanitized inside and out. You will be placing several inches of the tubing in your primary fermentation vessel, so it must be free from

bacteria and other contaminants! That means that during this process you only want it to touch things that have been cleaned and sanitized. I recommend keeping the spray bottle handy so that you can mist the inside of your sink and your work surface throughout the process.

3. Hold the tube with your thumb ready to close over one end of the tube. We're going to call this End A. Place End B under the faucet and turn it on. Try not to touch the hose to the actual faucet. Fill it completely with water from the tap. You'll need to play around with holding the ends at different levels. The goal is to get the tube filled completely, so I usually allow a little overflow before covering End A with my thumb. There should not be any empty space near end B.

4. When the tube is completely full, cover end B with your other thumb.

5. Place end A in your primary, still keeping end B covered.

6. If you are starting in the sink, uncover end B, and once the mead is close to end B, place end B as close to the bottom and side of your secondary as possible. (Some or even all of the water can go in your brew, but many people prefer to not add water at this point. I also think it's easier to get end B into the secondary when it's started in a bowl.)

7. If you are not starting in a sink, you can use the bowl to collect the water, and once it's flowing, get the tube into the bottom of the primary quickly.

8. Monitor the primary. Lower the tube in the primary to avoid getting air; even a little air is harmful to your end result. Don't go so low that you collect sediment.

Method #2: Using Your Mouth

You've seen it done in movies and cartoons and now you can try it for yourself. It's not as easy as it looks, but if you get the hang of starting the siphoning process with your mouth you'll stick with it because, in the long run, it's quicker and easier than the water method. The learning curve is rough and chances are you'll end up with water up your nose a few times. Call it "suffering for your art."

You'll need:

- Spray bottle of sanitizer solution
- Rubber tubing (thinner makes it easier)
- Your primary fermentation vessel
- Your secondary fermentation vessel, cleaned and sanitized
- A way to place your containers at two different heights

How to Do It:

1. Place your primary fermentation vessel higher than your secondary.
2. Make sure your tubing is completely sanitized. This method uses your mouth, one of the dirty parts of your body, so that spray bottle is going to come in handy. You'll also want to make sure you don't lick your lips right before siphoning.
3. Place one end of the tube in the primary fermentation vessel, well below the surface but nowhere near the sediment.
4. Place the other end of the tube in your mouth and suck gently.
5. When your mead is at about the halfway point in the tube, remove it from your mouth and place it in your secondary, at the bottom and side to minimize the possibility for splashing.
6. Monitor the tube in the primary, lowering it to avoid any air getting into the tube. Stop siphoning before you get to the sediment by lifting the end of the tube in the primary above the liquid.

This process is, seriously, a pain in the neck. I cannot advise enough that you practice a lot. Experiment with different tubing and heights for your primary and secondary to find the best method for you.

Here are a few things to consider. First, the more difference in height between the buckets, the better. Gravity is your friend. Your tube should be long enough that one end can rest on the bottom of your secondary, even as you move the tube in the primary down with the liquid. Too short and you risk losing some of your brew. Too long and the process won't work. Measure when you practice and place your containers in the same spot when you go through the process for real.

Try both methods and see if one is easier to you. Sticking to one method will be easier in the long run.

There is a tool that can help. You can purchase a racking cane (auto siphon is another name) from your local homebrew shop or online. There are two things to consider before purchasing one. Some do not fit in the neck of one-gallon carboys, and the racking cane is also tricky to learn to use. So no matter what, practice!

4. What Is Mead?

"Take rainwater kept for several years, and mix a sextarius of this water with a pound of honey. For a weaker mead, mix a sextarius of water with nine ounces of honey. The whole is exposed to the sun for forty days, and then left on a shelf near the fire. If you have no rain water, then boil spring water." —Columella

THE NECTAR OF the gods, mead, is a storied drink that, like many things in history, has been attributed to a group through popular culture references. In the case of mead, it is tied to the Vikings. These Scandinavian seafaring explorers who traversed the Atlantic are often pictured drinking the fermented honey from goblets. But the Vikings were most active between 700–1100 AD and Columella was writing about how to home-brew the drink nearly 700 years earlier. Believe it or not, mead is even older than that. It may, in fact, be the oldest alcoholic beverage on earth.

Each glass of mead you drink holds a long history. But what exactly is mead?

A Simple Recipe, a Complex Drink

At its core, mead is a fermented alcoholic beverage made from three ingredients: honey, water, and yeast. It was likely discovered by accident, as most alcoholic beverages were. Chances are, water that had sat in a hive and fermented with the help of airborne yeast was drunk. In addition to being tasty, the drinker likely felt pretty good. It was only a matter of time before the process was figured out so that man could make it for himself.[1]

When it comes to fermented alcoholic beverages, mead is most similar to wine. Just like a wine can be dry, sweet, or semisweet, and still or sparkling, so can a mead. Wine can be mixed with other spices, herbs, and fruits and, yes, so can mead.

Both wine and mead use three ingredients, two of which are water and yeast. But when making mead, the grapes are replaced with honey. One of the reasons people lose interest in mead is they assume that it can't be very complex or express itself in myriad ways. But they are wrong. And this is even more true when making mead at home. Mead is just as complex as wine, thanks to a few factors.

Think of a wine you enjoy. For me, it's Gewürztraminer. This white grape is grown in cooler climate wine regions like Alsace, Germany, and the Finger Lakes. While many are sweet and round, I find that I especially like semisweet or dry versions. My favorite, though, is the hard-to-find orange Gewürztraminer. This somewhat sour, somewhat tannic copper-hued wine is made with white grapes, but they are left in contact with the skins to impart both color and tannins into the final product. Most people don't believe it's a Gewürztraminer when they sip it. Many don't even believe it's wine. The complexity in a bottle of wine is borne of the varietal (grape), climate, when it was harvested, the fermentation temperature and vessel, how long the wine ages, and more. At the end of the day, there are limits. A Gewürztraminer will never be a Pinot Noir. But a Gewürztraminer can be many things, just like a Pinot Noir.

Mead is also expressed in many complex ways. The biggest influence on how a mead will taste is the type of honey used. If you've gotten used to getting your honey from the grocery store, possibly in a plastic bear, it's time to venture out and find local honey. And not just one local honey, but a few different types. Each will have its own

---

1   Slow Food Foundation for Biodiversity. "Khoisan Honey Mead." *https://www. fondazioneslowfood.com/en/ark-of-taste-slow-food/khoisan-honey-mead/.* n.p. n.d. Web.

unique color, consistency, and flavor. And these play a role in how your mead will turn out.

Type	Color	Consistency	Taste	Use
Alfalfa	White or light amber		Standard "honey" taste	
Avocado	Darker	Thicker	Rich Buttery	Dressings Sauces
Basswood	Watery white		Biting	
Blueberry	Light amber to amber		Full Round	Sauces Baking
Buckwheat	Dark brown	Thick	Strong Deep	BBQ Sauce Baking
Clover	Watery white to extra light	Thinner	Delicate	The most common honey; the one in your kitchen.
Sage	White or watery white		Sweet	Served with cheese
Sourwood			Sweet & Spicy	Table honey Glazes

[2]Buckwheat honey, which is not enjoyed by many people because of its strong taste, makes the perfect spiced mead. This thick, dark honey

---

2 Honey Colony. "17 Types of Honey And The Best Ways To Use Each Variety."
   www.honeycolony.com/article/17-types-of-honey/. n.p. n.d. Web. 17 Aug. 2017.

has a flavor similar to molasses and is not what most people think of when craving honey. That said, it makes a delicious base for spiced meads. Clover and orange blossom, however, are lighter and have a more subtle taste, perfect for a light, quaffable mead.

Varieties of Mead

There are a few different variations of mead, but for this book we will mostly focus on the traditional mead, which is simply honey, water, and yeast. We do include some pairing ideas that use other types of mead. You may wish to explore these after getting your basic recipe down. For each variety, the second ingredient is fermented with the honey in the same vessel, at the same time.

Melomel refers to any mead where the second ingredient is fruit. If apples are fermented with the honey, it's called cyser. When grapes are fermented with honey, it's called pyment. You can experiment with any range of fruit, though I particularly like those with strong flavors, such as citrus fruits.

Metheglin is mead that has spices, herbs, or both added to the honey to be fermented. This is an excellent way to make meads for different times of the year.

History of Mead

Imagine a plain near rivers. There, small communities live in single-room homes dug partially into the earth. They are simple people, reliant on farming and the breeding of animals to live. They supplement this with fish caught in nets, and hunt the area's deer and boar. These are the Jiahu of Neolithic China, a part of the larger Peiligang culture of prehistoric China. They are important because they created some of the region's earliest pottery, in which a beer/wine/mead hybrid was born.

Chances are that mead was actually discovered earlier, in Africa. Wild bees would store their honey in places that would fill with rainwater and then be collected. As people left the earliest human civilizations in Africa, they would have brought the knowledge of this honey water with them to other places, which could explain why we see early versions of mead in places like India and Europe. But China appears to be the first home of *intentional* mead-making.

Mead was first made in Northern China. We know this, thanks to Patrick McGovern of the University of Pennsylvania museum. McGovern and his team are responsible for analyzing preserved liquids from this period. The liquids remained because of the tight seals of the pottery.

McGovern discovered that the liquid was fermented from rice, honey, grapes, and hawthorn, a shrub. Molds were responsible for fermentation, which is a distinctly Chinese trait in fermented beverages. These core ingredients later found their way into beer, sake, mead, wine, and herbal wine. The early version of mead seen in China had many more ingredients than just honey, and was flavored with flowers such as chrysanthemums.

Why do we associate mead with the Vikings? Similarly to the ancient Africans discovering mead accidentally, the northern Europeans likely experienced a similar beautiful mistake. The northern Europeans kept bees in skeps, which are domed baskets that behave as hives. Unlike in modern hives with removable racks for taking honey, the bees had to be killed in order to get the honey. The best way to do this, they found, was by drowning the bees. The rinse water likely fermented into mead.

If mead has been around so long—possibly 40,000 years—why is it that we drink beer, wine, and spirits so much more frequently? Technology is to be blamed for mead's lack of popularity these days.

If we look at any civilization that made mead, we will find that the production and enjoyment dropped off significantly when technology advanced. The Industrial Revolution is a great example of this.

Before machines were used to extract honey, the first using centrifugal force, the combs were crushed. They were then rinsed, creating honey-infused rinse water that was fermented and enjoyed as mead. But as extraction advanced there was no need for the time consuming process of rinsing the comb and, because honey was expensive, mead production declined significantly.

Mead: The Most Sustainable Fermented Beverage?

As people become more aware of their consumption and its impact on the earth, mead is making a comeback. This is likely due to two concerns: honeybees and other resources.

Honeybees are gaining attention as their numbers drop significantly around the world. Beekeepers began noticing this in the 1990s. A diminished number of bees is cause for concern: bees are pollinators and help sustain crops. While "no farms, no food" is a great bumper sticker, the same could be applied to bees. They are necessary to human, animal, and plant life.

But the ethics of mead go beyond saving the bees and includes other resources. A vineyard, for example, requires substantial land, water, and fertilizer, and often a tremendous amount of energy is used. Turbines are used to control climate, machines are used for destemming and maceration, and so on.

Mead, though? It's one of the most primitive forms of brewing, requiring little to no human interaction, and does great things for the environment. Where there are bees, crops do well. From apples to flowers, bees spend their days collecting pollen and making honey. Mead is easy to make right in your kitchen with few ingredients—as the ancients proved, as little as honey and rain.

5. Brewing Your First Batch of Mead

MEAD IS AN excellent choice for starting your brewing adventures. It's one of the easiest, cheapest, least technical drinks to brew. It's also historical, sustainable, and delicious, so don't be put off by the ease and how little we as a drinking culture talk about mead.

I recommend beginning with a one-gallon batch of mead, which will give you about four wine bottles. It's not a lot, but it's enough to accomplish two goals important to a beginner. First, it will get you familiar with the process in a very controlled way. You're not going to be lugging around huge amounts of product and can focus on getting your technique down. Second, mead is best as it ages; by brewing a little at a time, you can get a good sense of how your particular batch ages by drinking and taking notes quarterly on your quality and amending your process each time. Ready to brew?

Basic Recipe for One-Gallon Batch of Mead

Equipment:
- 2 one-gallon carboys (glass)
- Air lock
- Solid rubber stopper
- Rubber stopper with hole
- Pot for heating water

- Metal or silicone skimming spoon (do not use a wooden spoon!)
- Funnel
- Immersion thermometer
- Rubber hose or auto siphon
- 4-6 beer bottles

Ingredients:
- 1 packet Lalvin D47 yeast
- 3 lbs unprocessed honey
- 1 gallon spring water
- ½ tsp yeast energizer
- 1 tsp yeast nutrient[3]

Process

The following steps are vital and contain a lot of information in order to help you understand the importance of every part of the process. Preparation is key when brewing mead, so do not skip any of these steps. A handy, abbreviated version follows on p. 32 for experienced brewers who understand some of these steps already from wine/cider/beer making and are starting their journey into mead.

Clean and Sanitize

1. Gather all equipment and ingredients.
2. Make sure to remove your yeast from the fridge so that it warms up to room temperature. This will take two to three hours; having it out a little longer is fine. Yeast is finicky so be sure it's ready.
3. Sanitize all equipment, following directions to the letter. See page 3 for an explanation of the difference between cleaning and sanitizing.

---

3   This is optional but will make your life much easier. You can buy some from the homebrew shop or use raisins, a little lemon juice, dead yeast, or epsom salts.

After your equipment is sanitized and rinsed, you'll prepare your ingredients.

Prepare Your Ingredients

1. Place your closed, sealed jar of honey in a sink of warm water. To ensure no water leaks into my jar, I leave it standing upright in water that comes about halfway up the jar and just swish it around now and again. This loosens the honey, making it easier to pour and use the entirety of the honey. It's not a necessary step, but it is efficient and ethical. No waste!

Make Your Must

1. It's time to brew! The first thing you want to do is pasteurize your water. No matter where you get your water from, there's stuff in it. You want to get most of that stuff out in order to maintain a pure flavor. Pasteurizing is easy, as you'll see below.
2. Bring ⅔ gallon water to a boil; immediately turn off heat. If you are using an electric stove, move it off the burner. It's now pasteurized.
3. Allow the water to cool for about fifteen minutes.
4. Add honey, yeast energizer, and yeast nutrient. This mixture of honey and water is called "must."
5. Stir the must well to blend the ingredients. As you do this, you'll likely get a white film on top. In my mead-making I create a whirlpool by stirring the must with a long spoon. This way, the film goes to the middle and I can easily scoop it away. Others who don't do this say their mead turns out fine.
6. Allow the must to sit for about ten minutes to cool down and rest.
7. Pour the must into the sanitized carboy using a sanitized funnel. Pop in the rubber stopper and airlock to keep

impurities out. Don't forget that those must be sanitized properly before being used.

8. Allow the must to cool down some more. The hardest part of the mead-making process is this wait. The next and final step is pitching your yeast, and you'll be eager to get there. But never forget that yeast is finicky. It will take several hours to get your must cooled down enough. Check the temperature hourly at first and then more frequently (read the section below for more information on the perfect temperature). If you don't have a thermometer, you want the bottom of the carboy to be slightly cool to the touch. If brewing in a temperature-controlled room, you can get away with leaving it overnight, but drafts, electric devices emanating heat, etc. will affect the temperature.

Pitching Yeast

Should you just toss the yeast in the must? Should you rehydrate? Only you can decide which method you like best, which you will discover over time. For your first batch, the key is to not shock the yeast by putting it in must that is too much warmer or colder than the yeast. Too cold and the yeast won't work as hard; too hot and you'll kill it.

If you look at your packet of yeast, it likely contains instructions. The best method for beginners is to remove the yeast from the fridge at the start of the process and allow it to slowly warm up to a warm room temperature. I like 72°F. Some people like 68°F. Try to stay between 70 and 75°F to encourage the yeast to do its stuff best.

This is another reason why starting with a one-gallon batch is smart. Most yeast packets are for five gallons, so you'll have plenty left to make another batch if you shock your yeast. But if you're patient and pay attention to detail, that is unlikely to happen.

While I'm not one for gadgets, you can get an immersion thermometer to monitor your temperature (one that is food safe and can be placed in water without breaking) for fewer than fifteen dollars.

1. *Aerate your must.* That yeast needs oxygen to work to its best potential, so agitate your must before adding yeast. There's no need for a fancy stirring plate. I generally use a hand whisk or small handheld electric mixer, but your stirring spoon is fine. Whatever you use, make sure you sanitize it first. Stir for about two minutes, changing direction if you're using a spoon. You can also put the cap from the carboy back on (make sure to sanitize it first!) and shake the carboy for two minutes.

2. *Pitch your yeast.* For your first batch, use about half of your yeast packet, or two-and-a-half grams. Just put it into the must and then give the carboy a good shake. Put the rubber stopper and airlock back in place and move the carboy to where the magical fermentation can happen.

First Ferment

Fermentation is where your must becomes mead and, as hard as it is, it's important to leave it alone as much as possible. Fermentation works best at a stable temperature and in a place without direct sunlight. Thanks to brewing a one-gallon batch, you can ferment in a closet or even a cupboard, depending on your home's layout. If you can't find a place without sun, wrap your carboy in towels, sheets, or your favorite concert tee. Just keep the sun from wreaking havoc on your process.

It will take anywhere from a few hours to two days for evidence of fermentation to appear. You'll notice bubbles in the airlock and activity in the carboy. This means your yeast is doing the job and in six to twelve months you're going to have some mead. That's right. Mead is quick to get to fermentation, but the fermentation process takes a long time.

In the beginning you'll have a lot of bubbles. I like to check on my mead every other day and count how many bubbles per second. Eventually this will slow down to about one bubble per minute. It may even stop completely. Once it has slowed considerably, it's time to rack your mead.

Racking

Racking is a fancy term for moving your mead from primary to secondary fermentation. This is done with a siphoning hose or an auto siphon. Personally, I'm a fan of the auto siphon, and that's because of oxygen.

Oxygen is great before pitching yeast. In fact, it's imperative. But once mead starts fermenting, oxidation will result in significant flaws, including mead that tastes like cardboard. Don't move the carboy much, or at all, if possible. And when it comes to racking, you want as few splashes as possible.

1. Transfer the mead into a freshly sanitized glass carboy using a hose or auto siphon. Leave as much sediment behind as possible.
2. Put the stopper and airlock on the new container. You shouldn't see much activity, but sometimes you'll see a few bubbles.
3. Wait. Yes, we're waiting again. Secondary fermentation is aging, and mead is best enjoyed when aged a long time. If this is your first time, consider bottling at three months and tasting quarterly to see how you like it. You can start a new batch right away and age six months or a year or more. Keep accurate notes to see which versions you like best.

Bottling/Kegging

After secondary fermentation, or aging, for at least three months, it will be time to bottle your mead. You will end up with four to six beer bottle-sized bottles. Larger batches of mead can be kegged.

Use an auto siphon to carefully move mead from secondary to the bottles. Cap each as it's filled.

Be sure to take a taste of the mead prior to bottling so that you can get a sense of its complete journey! And don't forget, mead gets better with age, so let some bottles sit so you can see how the flavor changes over time.

Simplified Brewing Instructions

At some point you're going to become a pro, or maybe you already know all the terminology as an experienced home brewer or wine-maker. In that case, here are the streamlined instructions:

Step	Equipment/ Ingredients	Why	Notes
Sanitation	Pot, carboy, both stoppers, airlock, spoon, funnel, honey in sealed glass jar.	Avoid flaws and corruption	Follow all directions and be careful; sanitizer is nasty stuff. Get the honey runny so it's easy to pour and you don't waste any.
Remove yeast from fridge	Yeast	Get it up to appropriate pitch temperature	If you forget to do this, do it as soon as you remember. Your must can sit out a little longer since you're pitching around room temp.
Boil	Pot, ⅔ gallon water	Need to pasteurize, but you don't want to lose too much to evaporation.	If you're using an electric stove, move your pot off the burner.
Cool for about 15 minutes			
Make your must	3 lbs honey, pot, water, yeast energizer, and nutrient, if using		Make sure your whisk/ spoon/stirrer was cleaned and sanitized! You're below boiling temp now.
Place in primary	Must, glass carboy	Your must is ready to move to its new home.	Use a cleaned, sanitized funnel.
Cool		Yeast needs the bath water to be just right.	This can take hours, so pop in a solid stopper or stopper with hole/ airlock and distract yourself.

Continued on next page . . .

| Pitch yeast | ½ packet of yeast | Aerate your must first by shaking, pouring into something sanitized and back, etc. | |
| Primary fermentation | | Wrap in a tee shirt or black garbage bag if your must will sit in direct sunlight for any time. | |

Sustainable Mead

Brewing mead is a great way to support your local environment and your local bees and beekeeper. At the same time, it is a tremendous waste of water. This batch of one gallon will waste ten gallons of water during the cleaning/sanitizing process. There are ways to mitigate this, though.

Never, ever skip cleaning and sanitizing. Failing to take these steps will result in a flawed batch that you'll dump down the drain, resulting in eleven gallons of wasted water. Luckily, there are ways to reduce the amount of wasted water by repurposing household water before, during, and after brewing.

Prior to brewing, you will have to clean and sanitize your equipment. Each of these steps requires about five gallons of water for a one-gallon batch of mead. But you can cut down on this considerably. It just takes some planning, and thinking outside the box.

The water you're using to clean your equipment needs to be hot. Instead of running the tap and watching gallons drain away before it gets hot, boil the water. Allow it to cool to 100-120°F, pour it into your stopped sink, add your powdered brewing wash, and follow the directions on the container. Sounds weird, I know, but this water is just for cleaning, and boiling it is going to kill anything living in it. The detergent will take care of the rest. You're also going to sanitize your equipment after cleaning, which will kill everything even thinking about taking up residence on your tools.

You just went from more than five gallons wasted to zero gallons wasted. Now, do the same for sanitizing and you'll have saved even more.

If you're really ambitious, you can boil rainwater and use it as your brewing water. Boiling water often makes it safer than tap water, but some people get nervous about collecting rainwater because of the things they have to skim off. I get that. Using a fine mesh screen over your barrel is a great way to keep debris out of your water.

In addition to making ethical choices about water use when brewing mead, there are other ways to be conscious of your consumption. One way is by carefully selecting the honey you use. Honey is an ethical dilemma. Most vegans refrain because they do not engage in the consumption of anything produced by animals. Others, however, believe that if the honey is produced ethically, it's fine. Bees produce far more honey, wax, and propolis than they need.

So, how do you know if honey is ethical? When I started my journey into more ethical consumption, I assumed that if I bought honey from someone who kept their own hives I could check the "ethical" box and move along. Turns out that's not the case. Here's how to approach purchasing honey if you wish to be ethical in your mead-making.

First, if it is mass-produced, it's not ethical. Bees are stacked in huge hives and essentially worked to death to produce commercial honey. Part of this is nature: bees work in order to survive and will try to fill the hive. They don't have the capacity to understand that it is a large hive with extra bees. Part is nurture: commercial honey producers want to produce as much honey as possible on as small a budget as possible. That's fine for them; I understand that capitalism is not going anywhere any time soon. It's not fine for me.

In addition to commercial honey being the product of a terrible life for the bees making it, it doesn't taste nearly as good. The bees are kept in a smaller area with limited places to collect pollen, thus diminishing the flavor.

Find local honey. That's the first step to being ethical. Chances are you live near someone who has a few hives and sells honey. Just take a drive in the country and you're likely to find signs on the side of the road advertising fresh honey. Where I live, these little stands populate the dirt roads; many aren't even manned. Leave the money, take the honey—add this to your list of proof that yes, Vermont *is* as idyllic as you thought. If you happen to find a manned stand, ask if you can see the hives. Most beekeepers love to show their hives as well as the plants the bees are visiting. And this is what you want: bees that are free to zoom around and check things out, selecting which plants they visit.

If you're further along in your journey toward sustainability and more ethical consumption, ask the beekeeper if she loans out her bees. This is where things get dicey for many people. It's where I recently drew the line in my acquiring of ingredients. Some bee-keepers put their hives and bees on tractor-trailers and ship them down south or even to California to help with almond crops. This makes a lot of sense and keeps cross-pollination alive and well. On the other hand, it is creating a large carbon footprint and exhausts and stresses the bees. I, personally, stick to local bees who get to live as natural a life as possible.

No matter how strict you are in your approach to ingredients, there are benefits to choosing local honey versus commercial, not the least of which is the difference in flavor.

6. Mead Flavors, Recipes, and Pairing Suggestions

ONCE YOU MAKE one batch of mead you'll be hooked. As you develop your base recipe, chances are the urge will strike to venture into other types of mead. There are a few different ways to do this.

Like grape wine, mead ranges from dry to sweet. For a one gallon batch like the starter recipe in this book, one and a half to two pounds of honey makes a light colored, dry mead; three pounds results in a semi-sweet mead; and three and a half to four pounds will produce a sweet mead. Pay attention to the strain of yeast you use. If you want a very dry mead, use Lalvin EC-1118 yeast. For semisweet and sweet meads, Lalvin 47 is your best choice. This yeast is user-friendly and imparts great flavor that complements the honey.

The type of honey used influences the flavor of mead (see chapter 1). Traditional mead is best made using alfalfa, clover, acacia, or wildflower honey. Acacia honey will sweeten even the driest of meads and is a great option if you're going crazy-dry. Just remember that crazy-dry means even more finicky yeast.

Most mead takes a long time to make, which means that as you make batches throughout the year, you can play with the flavors through honey, yeast, and additions. Save your flavored meads for the right season and pair them to impress your friends. Mead is best after aging. Make batches throughout the year using fresh items that will pack the peak of flavor into each delicious gallon.

When it comes to types of mead, there are styles that are not flavored in the secondary, but from the start. I've broken down a few of the most popular here with seasonal suggestions. You can find one recipe for each in the recipes chapter at the end of this section.

Mead through the Seasons

You can make any mead at any time of year, but these seasonal suggestions are fun to make at the right time of year and to drink the following year. Aging mead for a year gives it a richness and complexity that will have you coming back for more.

Winter

Bochet (sometimes spelled "bouchet," see recipe on page 43) is mead made with honey that is caramelized or burned before it is added to the water. The browned honey expresses several flavors including toffee, chocolate, and marshmallow. This is enjoyable on its own or flavored with spices and fruit. Try adding nutmeg, cinnamon, or orange peel for a delightful winter brew. One of the things I love most about making bochet is that the spices can be used multiple times. While you don't need a cauldron to make it, the following recipe from the fourteenth century will give you a sense of the allure of this drink.

"BOUCHET. To make six sesters of bouchet, take six pints of fine sweet honey, and put it in a cauldron on the fire and boil it, and stir continually until it starts to grow, and you see that it is producing bubbles like small globules which burst, and as they burst emit a little smoke which is sort of dark: and then stir, and then add seven sixths of water and boil until it reduces to six sixths again, and keep stirring. And then put it in a tub to cool until it is just warm; and then strain it through a cloth bag, and then put it in a cask and add one chopine (half-litre) of beer-yeast, for it is this which makes it the most piquant, (and if you use bread yeast, however much you like the taste, the colour will be insipid), and cover it well and warmly to work. And if you want to make it very good, add an ounce of ginger, long pepper, grains of Paradise and cloves in equal amounts, except for the cloves of which there should be less, and put them in a cloth bag and throw in. And after two or three days, if the bouchet smells spicy enough and is strong enough, take out the spice-bag and squeeze it and put it in the next barrel you make. And thus you will be able to use these same spices three or four times." —Le Menagier de Paris, France, 1393

Spring

Moral (see recipe on page 44) means melomel (mead that also contains fruit) made from mulberries. This is a delicate flavor perfect for spring. White and red mulberries are ready for picking in late spring. You can find them at the farmers' market or forage for them, depending on where you live. As children growing up, we picked them straight from the trees on the side of the road.

Rhodomel (see recipe on page 49) is mead from rosehips; it gets its name from the ancient Romans who enjoyed it. Rosehips, containing roses' seeds, are a popular ingredient in tea, fresh and tart with a taste similar to hibiscus. They are harvested from rose bushes in the fall but should be drunk in the summer. Mead needs time to age, so making a batch when they are harvested and waiting over a year is your best bet.

Spring means maple syrup and maple syrup means acerglyn (recipe on page 45). This mead requires plenty of time to age, but it's worth it. Choose *Grade A: Dark Color & Robust Flavor* (which is what used to be called Grade B).

Summer

Some like it hot! If that's you, you should brew capsicumel, mead flavored with chili pepper (see recipe on page 46). Capsicumel is unexpected and delightful. Chili peppers will make it to the farmers' market in late summer, but they are also easy to grow at home. This is a trickier recipe, so get a few plain batches under your belt before breaking out the chilies.

Morat made from black mulberries can be made in summer, usually late summer (see recipe on page 44). You'll get gorgeous color and

subtle flavor from mulberries, creating a drink that is a little sweet and has berry notes. Morat is one of the best meads to drink young, so if you're not patient and are ready to move from basic mead to melomel, this is the first recipe to try.

If you like lemonade, you'll love sima (see recipe on page 48). This is the Finnish take on mead and it is seasoned with lemons. Lemons are available year round, and the Finns traditionally drink this for May Day. I prefer this flavor in summer, like lemonade. It's important to know that sima has a very low alcohol content, so if you're making a traditional recipe, like the one I've included, be sure to drink it fairly quickly before it turns. This is a fizzy, refreshing mead that you'll find yourself making regularly.

Fall

Cyser is—you guessed it—mead made with apples or apple juice. This is an interesting way to enjoy a twist on cider. It can be made in fall during harvest and enjoyed any time of year, but of course fall and winter are best.

Recipes

Below you'll find a one-gallon recipe for each type of mead recommended above, starting with the difficulty level and followed by the equipment and ingredients. From there you'll find the flavor profile, followed by possible spice additions. (See the supplement on how to flavor your meads.) Finally, find pairing suggestions for when you crack open and enjoy your mead.

Bochet

Level:	Intermediate to advanced
Equipment:	Very large pot for boil (four- to five-gallon capacity)
	Primary and secondary fermentation vessels
	Plug with hole
	Airlock
	Plug with no hole
	Stirring spoon
	Gloves
	Goggles or other protective eyewear
Ingredients:	1.4 gallons water
	2–3 lbs honey (local, but cheap)
	1 packet Lalvin EC-1118 or Lalvin D-47 yeast
	1 tsp yeast nutrient
	½ tsp yeast energizer
Flavor profile:	toasted marshmallow, maple, slightly bitter, vanilla
Spices:	allspice, anise, cardamom, cinnamon, cloves, ginger, nutmeg, vanilla

Process:

1. Pour one gallon of your brew water into the pot and mark where the water hits.
2. Pour the water out.
3. Pour the honey into the pot and heat over medium-high heat. Stir as the honey heats. It will bubble and expand

considerably. *Honey is extremely hot and volatile. Once the boil starts, turn down the heat so that it is boiling, but not splattering out of the pot.*

4. When the honey forms bubbles that spit steam when they burst, remove from heat. You can't turn off the heat too early, so err on the side of caution as you start out.
5. Put on gloves and goggles.
6. Add water to the honey carefully—the mixture will splatter.
7. Continue to boil until the must reduces to one gallon, as marked on your pot in Step 1.
8. Pour into carboy, add yeast, and continue as in the base recipe in chapter 5 (start at step 4 under "Make Your Must," page 28).

Pairing Suggestions:

Entrée:	Roasted duck with ginger glaze
Charcuterie Board:	Brie, cheddar, apple, dried fruits, pancetta, prosciutto, pistachios
Dessert:	Crème brûlée

Morat

Level:	Novice
Equipment:	Pot
	Primary and secondary fermentation vessels
	Plug with hole
	Airlock
	Plug with no hole
	Stirring spoon
Ingredients:	2 lbs honey (local, but cheap)
	1 gallon water, divided
	1/2 tsp yeast nutrient
	1 packet Lalvin D-47 yeast
	3 lbs mulberries (cleaned, sorted, frozen; thawed overnight and crushed the night before racking to secondary)

Process:

1. Combine honey, a half gallon of water, and yeast nutrient. Heat to 160°F and maintain for thirty minutes. Skim and remove any foam that collects.

2. Remove from heat and cool to 80°F. Funnel into your one-gallon glass carboy and pitch the yeast according to directions. Pop on your airlock.

3. Fermentation should start within a few days. When it has slowed, siphon into your secondary. Add thawed, crushed mulberries.

4. Put the airlock back in and monitor. When fermentation stops, rack again and store for two to four months.

Pairing Suggestions:

Entrée:	Fried flounder with apricot sauce
Charcuterie Board:	Brie, mild goat cheese, quince paste, dried fruits, turkey, chicken, macadamia nuts
Dessert:	Dark chocolate mousse

Acerglyn

Level:	Intermediate
Equipment:	Pot
	Primary and secondary fermentation vessels
	Plug with hole
	Airlock
	Plug with no hole
	Stirring spoon
Ingredients:	2 to 2½ lbs light honey (I used clover)
	2 quarts maple syrup
	Acid to taste (no more than 1 tsp; refer to page 124 for more info on measuring ABV)
	Pasteur champagne yeast

Directions:

1. Bring honey and maple syrup to boil in enough water to liquefy.
2. Add acid.
3. Skim for a minute or two.
4. Cool to at least 70°F.
5. Add water to make your must. Should have a starting gravity of 1.120 (refer to pages 124–127).
6. Pitch with working Pasteur champagne yeast. Should have moderate-vigorous fermentation.
7. Rack off after primary fermentation, and once again if it isn't clear in a few more weeks.
8. If the yeast isn't settling after the first fermentation, top off carboy with boiled water.

Pairing Suggestions:

Entrée: Grilled skirt steak with charred zucchini and pineapple salad

Charcuterie Board: Aged Gouda, aged cheddar, cranberries, dates, hard salami, andouille sausage

Dessert: Brie and apple tart with caramel drizzle

Capsicumel[4]

Level: Advanced

Equipment: Pot

Primary and secondary fermentation vessels

Plug with hole

Airlock

Plug with no hole

Stirring spoon

---

4   The Winemaking Home Page. "Requested Recipe: Capsicumel (Capsimel) [Chile Mead]." *http://winemaking.jackkeller.net/request196.asp.* n.p. n.d. Web. Sep. 30 2003.

Rubber gloves

Straining bags

Ingredients: 2½ lbs light honey, divided

7½ pts water

16 medium-sized jalapeños (for less heat,
   use 8 jalapeños)

1 lb golden raisins, chopped or minced

1½ tsp acid blend

¼ tsp grape tannin

¾ tsp yeast nutrient

½ tsp pectic enzyme

1 packet Pasteur champagne yeast

½ tsp potassium sorbate

Campden tablet, crushed

Directions:

1. Mix 2 lbs honey into water and bring to boil. Boil twenty minutes, skimming off any scum that forms.

2. While boiling, wear rubber gloves to wash jalapeños and cut off stems. Slice lengthwise and remove seeds. Place peppers in blender or food chopper with two cups water and chop coarsely. Set aside.

3. Chop or mince raisins. Put raisins in nylon straining bag and, over primary, pour chopped jalapeños in with raisins. Tie bag and leave in primary.

4. Add acid blend, tannin, and yeast nutrient.

5. Pour honey water over ingredients and stir. Cover primary and set aside until room temperature.

6. When room temperature, add pectic enzyme, cover, and set aside twelve hours.

7. Add yeast and cover.

8. Stir daily until vigorous fermentation subsides (seven to ten days). Wearing rubber gloves, squeeze nylon bag over

primary, then discard contents of bag. Transfer liquid to secondary, top up, and fit airlock.

9. Ferment to absolute dryness (sixty to ninety days). Rack into clean secondary, top up, and refit airlock.

10. Rack twice more, forty-five days apart.

11. Stabilize with potassium sorbate and crushed Campden tablet (stirred well), wait fourteen days, then add ½ cup of light, clear honey and stir well to dissolve. Taste. If heat is too strong, add ¼ cup of honey and stir well. Taste again. Add additional honey if required.

12. Wait another thirty days and rack into bottles. Age at least six months. Will improve to two years.

Pairing Suggestions:

Entrée:	Avocado, fennel, grapefruit, and papaya salad
Charcuterie Board:	Macadamia nuts, walnuts, red berries, salami, prosciutto, manchego, Brie, blue cheese
Dessert:	Oatmeal cookies with macadamia nuts, dark chocolate, and coconut

Sima[5]

Level:	Novice
Equipment:	Pot
	Primary and secondary fermentation vessels
	Plug with hole
	Airlock
	Plug with no hole
	Stirring spoon
Ingredients:	1¼ gallons boiling water
	2–3 lemons

---

5 Storm The Castle. "Make Sima (Finnish Mead)." *www.stormthecastle.com/mead/make-sima-finnish-mead.htm.* n.p n.d. Web. Northern Brewer. "Sparkling Spring Sima for Vappu (May Day)." https://www.northernbrewer.com/connect/2010/04/sparking-spring-sima-for-vappu-may-day/ n.p. n.d. Web.

½ cup white sugar

½ cup brown sugar

½ tsp dry Premier Cuvée yeast

3 raisins per bottle (at bottling)

Directions:

1. Bring water to a boil.
2. As water heats, scrub the lemons. Grate the zest from the lemons and set it aside in a small bowl.
3. Peel or cut off the pith (the white part of the peel). Slice or chop the flesh of the lemons, removing the seeds as you go, and add to the bowl of zest.
4. When the water is boiling, reduce the heat and add the sugars and lemon parts. Stir until sugar is fully dissolved.
5. Remove from heat and let sit until room temperature.
6. Transfer everything to your fermenter, including the lemon flesh and zest. Add yeast.
7. Seal with an airlock and leave at room temperature for forty-eight hours.
8. Fill each bottle and add raisins.
9. When the raisins rise to the top of the liquid, the sima is ready to drink.

Pairing Suggestions:

Entrée: Grilled chicken or tofu with mango thyme chutney

Charcuterie Board: Almonds, pistachios, goat cheese, fresh buffalo mozzarella, prosciutto, serrano ham

Dessert: Tippaleipä

Rhodomel

Level: Novice

Equipment: Pot

Primary and secondary fermentation vessels

Plug with hole

Airlock

Plug with no hole

Stirring spoon

Ingredients: 15 lbs alfalfa honey

1 gallon water, divided

1.5 pint dried rose petals

¼ tsp citric acid

½ tsp tannin

1 tsp yeast nutrient

1 packet champagne yeast

Directions:

1. Boil honey and one quart of water for ten minutes, skimming off foam.
2. Place petals, citric acid, and tannin in a one-gallon glass carboy. Use the funnel to add the honey water.
3. Add water to make one gallon. When the must is between 75°F and 80°F, add nutrient, sprinkle the yeast on top of the must, and put the airlock on the top of the carboy. Allow to sit for seven to ten days.
4. After seven to ten days, siphon the must into another carboy and ferment until clear.
5. Bottle and age for at least six months.

Pairing Suggestions:

Entrée: Honey roasted chicken with carrots

Charcuterie Board: Almonds, pecans, hazelnuts, Brie, blue cheese, mascarpone, grilled chicken, honey turkey

Dessert: Strawberry marzipan bars

Cyser

Level: Novice

Equipment: 1 gallon glass carboy

Airlock

Stopper with hole

Ingredients: 1½ lbs clover honey

1½ lbs wildflower honey

1 gallon cider

2 Campden tablets

1 packet ale yeast

Directions:

1. Mix everything except the yeast.
2. Let sit in fermenter with airlock for twenty-four hours.
3. Add yeast.
4. Rack to secondary when fermentation slows.
5. Bottle.
6. Allow to age at least three months. Six months of aging is optimal.

Pairing Suggestions:

Entrée: Grilled lemon oregano chicken or lamb, Indian food

Charcuterie Board: Aged cheddar, aged Gouda, goat cheese, spiced mixed nuts, pepperoni, Soppressata, raisins

Dessert: Lemon pound cake

The Buzz About Honeybees

There's been a lot of buzz about the honeybee population for years now. Why are people so interested, what are the facts, and why does it matter?

There are several types of bees—stinging and sting-less—that make honey, but the one we're most familiar with is the Western honeybee or *apis mellifera* (honey-bearing bee).[6] It is the most common bee in the world, having originated in tropical eastern Africa, and present on every continent except Antarctica.

The bee population faces significant threats. In 2016 one third of the colonies in the US died. One major reason is the use of pesticides in large-scale commercial farming. This heralds risk to humans. One bite of every three we take is a result of bee pollination, which means, essentially, that one third of our food source is at risk right along with the bees. Despite this, humans continue to create significant threats to the bee population.

---

6   Michael S. Engel (1999). "The taxonomy of recent and fossil honey bees (Hymenoptera: Apidae: Apis)". Journal of Hymenoptera Research. 8: 165–196.

Are all bees fated to die? Hopefully not. Growing awareness and intervention from the EPA and USDA, as well as major
funding from universities for studies, helps. This macro-
awareness leads to precaution and could lead to major changes
on a legislative or regulatory level. On the micro-level, though,
change is also important. There are ways everyone can help the
bee population.

7. What Is Cider?

It seemed I was a mite of sediment
That waited for the bottom to ferment
So I could catch a bubble in ascent.
I rode up on one till the bubble burst,
And when that left me to sink back reversed
I was no worse off than I was at first.
I'd catch another bubble if I waited.
The thing was to get now and then elated.
—"In A Glass of Cider" by Robert Frost

IT'S NOT SURPRISING that Robert Frost, a famous Vermonter, wrote a poem about cider. New England, with its incredible fiery autumns, is cider country. But just as Frost came from elsewhere to love Vermont and make it his home, cider is not native to Vermont, New England, or even the Northeast of the United States. The earliest written record of cider comes from the Romans. They drank cider during the 55 BC invasion of Britain, and the record shows that Caesar was a fan. Cider remained popular in England. In the Middle Ages it was the favored beverage because the water was dangerous to drink.

William Blackstone brought apple seeds with him to the colonies and is credited with planting the first orchards around 1623. Apples took off in Vermont. The state, in the early 1800s, had 125 distilleries and, like in England centuries before, bad water made the drink a desired commodity.

Despite the huge popularity of cider, it eventually lost favor. Orchards required far more land, time, and resources than the beer recipe Germans brought with them, and the rising desire to ban alcohol in the 1800s, which would become a reality in 1920, didn't help cider's plight, either. Orchards were burned, many of which were never replanted.

From Tree to Tankard

Hard cider is the result of fermenting sweet apple cider. It can be made very simply and quickly with just some store-bought sweet apple cider, water, and yeast. It only takes about eight weeks from tree to tankard, with bottling at the halfway point. It's also incredibly cheap to make; a gallon of cider can be purchased for fewer than five dollars. For these reasons, cider is a great starter for home brewers. The lower price per batch allows you to perfect your yeast pitching, working out your process and playing with carbonation at a far lower cost per batch than mead.

While drunk like beer, and often served alongside it in bars and restaurants, cider is more similar in process to wine and mead. That is not to say, though, that it is not just as diverse and malleable as beer. Cider can be made from a variety of apples, not just traditional cider apples, which changes everything from texture to flavor. Additionally, it can be made sweet, semisweet, or dry, and still or sparkling. It's easy to make sparkling cider at home—it just requires a few extra steps at bottling.

Cider making is an environmentally friendly choice because there is an abundance of apples, including types we don't generally eat, that work well in cider. You can buy a fancier, single varietal juice and make a single or mixed varietal cider, you can press your own mix of apples, or use cider from the local orchard and see what turns out. Additionally, you can use older apples that have started to shrivel or have spots. The only thing that must be avoided is rot. If you choose to pick and press your own apples, cut away rotten spots or you'll infect your batch.

Another reason cider is the preference of ethical brewers is that apples that would normally not get eaten, the awful bitter ones, make the best ciders. This reduces waste.

For the purpose of quick-brewing, this book includes recipes that use non-alcoholic cider as the main ingredient. If you are interested in pressing your own cider or working with a local orchard to have cider pressed for you, see The Anatomy of Cider (page 72).

Terroir in Cider-Making

Terroir is the difficult-to-define influence that soil, climate, seasonal temperatures, and coastal waters have on the flavor of a wine. It's geographic. It's geologic. It's why you might love one Pinot Noir and hate another: the grape is really just a vehicle for terroir. And it doesn't just influence oenology.

You're likely not going to hear someone tasting a cider like they do a wine, with a discussion of region and the peculiarities of a particularly good vintage despite drought or rot. But those who work closely with apples have been well aware of the influence of what can only be called terroir. In his 1846 *Fruits and Fruit Trees of America*, Andrew Jackson Downing made the footnote, "It is well to remark that many of the so-called new varieties, especially from the West, prove to be old and well-known kinds, slightly altered in appearance by new soil and different climate." It's not nearly as pronounced as in grapes, but apples are also influenced by terroir, or "place."

There's a Place for Place in Cider

Where we can apply terroir, and where it is important to ethical brewers, is that it reminds us of the importance of using local ingredients. Ciders made by us or our neighbors or that come from local orchards are the most ethical.

When buying local cider (or local apples to make cider), we support local farms, cut down on transportation, and help our local honeybee population. This, and the fact that cider is quick and easy to brew, makes it the perfect choice for home brewers who are interested in greening up their process, or new brewers who want to switch to conscious, eco-friendly brewing.

8. Brewing Your First Batch of Cider

BREWING CIDER IS similar to brewing mead, so you shouldn't need to buy additional equipment. Some of the ingredients also overlap. Here's what you need to brew a one-gallon batch of cider, which yields about four wine bottles or ten beer bottles.

Basic Cider Recipe

Equipment:

- 1-gallon carboy with cap
- Funnel
- Stopper with airlock
- Hydrometer
- Fermometer (stick-on thermometer)
- Bottle filler

- 3 feet plastic tubing
- Auto-siphon racking cane
- Bottle capper
- 10 caps (never reuse)
- 10 bottles (save empties)

Ingredients:
- 1 oz Campden tablets
- 1 gallon apple juice (press local apples fresh yourself for the best results)
- 1 oz pectic enzyme[7]
- ½ tsp champagne yeast[8] (feel free to experiment once you get the process down)
- 1 oz organic corn sugar[9]
- ½ cup water

Starter Recipe:[10]

1. The night prior to brewing, crush a Campden tablet in about a tablespoon of water and set aside.
2. Prepare a clean working area in the room where you brew.
3. Clean and sanitize your equipment.
4. Use your funnel to pour one gallon of room temperature apple juice into your glass carboy. See the tips on page 61 for information on purchasing a one-gallon glass jug of apple juice.
5. If your juice is unfiltered, add one ounce of pectic enzyme. You can skip this step if you start with clear apple juice or don't mind a hazy look.

---

7   If you want a clear cider you will use pectic enzyme. You can skip it if you don't mind a hazy, unfiltered look to your cider.
8   I recommend Lalvin EC-1118; it is forgiving when it comes to temperature. See Understanding Yeast (p. 128) to get to know yeast. It's the key to successful brewing.
9   If you don't want carbonated hard cider you can skip this.
10 Mountain Feed and Farm Supply. "How To Brew Hard Cider: Start With A 1-Gallon Kit." *www.moutainfeed.com/blogs/learn/16290877-how-to-brew-hard-cider-start-with-a-1-gallon-kit*. n.p. n.d. Web.

6. Add crushed Campden tablet.

7. Float 1/4 to 1/2 a teaspoon of champagne yeast on top of the juice for a few minutes. This should activate the yeast. After at least three minutes, swirl the bottle to mix. If you wish, place the *sanitized* cap on the bottle to give it a good shake. Just make sure it's sanitized!

8. Place the sanitized stopper and airlock on the carboy.

9. If you haven't already, place the Fermometer on the outside of the carboy. Place the jug in a warm place where it is shielded from light and able to stay warm, preferably between 55 and 75°F.

10. Allow to sit, mostly undisturbed, for thirty days. During the first week you should see lots of activity: the liquid will churn and foam and your airlock will be bubbling. It's okay if this doesn't last a full week. If you don't see activity, consider activating and pitching a little extra yeast.

11. After thirty days, check the airlock. There should be little to no activity (one bubble or fewer per five-minute span). If you're seeing little to no activity, it's time to bottle. If you wish to make sparkling cider, continue with step 12. Otherwise, skip to step 14.

12. Boil corn sugar in 1/2 cup of water for about 5 minutes or until completely dissolved. Cool to 70°F.

13. Add cooled sugar solution to carboy and swirl gently to mix evenly. Gentle swirling for longer is better than vigorous swirling; you don't want to stir up too much yeast from the bottom of the carboy.

14. Sanitize your bottles, caps, bottle capper, tubing, auto siphon, and bottle filler.

15. Connect one end of your tubing to the bottle filler and the other to the auto siphon.

16. Fill bottles, being careful to keep the siphon above the sediment at the bottom of the carboy.

17. Store for three to six months before sampling, especially if you carbonate your cider.

Tips

- Campden tablets are dangerous to those with a sulfite allergy. Be sure to label bottles you give as gifts, and let any guests know that your cider has sulfites. That said, Campden tablets are vital to the brewing process, so do not skip this step! If sulfites are an issue, stick to mead.

- Siphoning is hard. There are no shortcuts. Practice siphoning water on non-brewing days until you get the hang of it.

- You don't have to clarify cider by using pectic enzyme; it's purely aesthetic. I skip pectic enzyme and keep my brews hazy. Maybe it's because I love an unfiltered beer. No, it's probably because I'm cheap. If you are preparing cider for a competition, clarifying is an easy way to gain two points. Or if you're photographing your cider in really gorgeous glassware, you may want it clear. Do what works for you.

- If you can, buy your apple juice in a glass jug. Then you only have to use a spray of sanitizer instead of doing a full clean/ sanitize. Just make sure you do it well.

9. Types of Cider and Cider Recipes

CIDER CAN BE made from a range of apple varieties and with a variety of methods to produce different flavors.[11] Play around with them to see what you like, and then the sky's the limit! You can mix and match varieties, steep herbs, add other fruit, or, if you want to jump on the latest trend, hop your cider. The following table includes just some of the many variations you can make.

Types of Cider

Cyser	Made by fermenting honey and apple juice; considered a type of mead.
Draft Cider	Still cider that usually has an ABV (alcohol by volume) of 6% or less.
Farmhouse Style/ Scrumpy	Cider made using traditional methods, fermented without additional sugars. Unfiltered, non-carbonated. No additives and no added yeast, only that which is found on the apples naturally. Strong, tannic, and an ABV of 6–8%.
French Style	Cider made using a fermentation called keeving. Also called *Cidre*, this style is sweeter, fruitier, and lower in alcohol. Typical ABV is as low as 2% and not higher than 5%.
Ice Cider	Crazy-sweet cider made from apples or juice frozen prior to fermentation. Very sweet and acidic with no tannic quality.
Perry	Cider made from pear and apple juice.
Wood-Aged	Cider that is aged in barrels or casks imparting flavors similar to those found in oaked wine: smoke, vanilla, spice.

---

11   Liquorcraft. "Cider". www.liquorcraft.com.au/websiles/Liquorcraft/files/ Cider.pdf. n.p. n.d. Web.

Cider Recipes

Cyser (A Cider/Mead Hybrid)

Level: Novice

Equipment: 1 gallon glass carboy

                 Airlock

                 Stopper with hole

Ingredients: 1½ lbs clover honey

                 1½ lbs wildflower honey

                 1 gallon cider

                 2 Campden tablets

                 1 packet ale yeast

Directions

1. Mix everything except the yeast.
2. Let sit in fermenter with airlock in a warm, dark location for twenty-four hours.
3. Add yeast.
4. Rack to secondary when fermentation slows.
5. Bottle.
6. Allow to bottle age for at least three months. Six months is ideal.

Pairing Suggestions:

Entrée: Grilled lemon oregano chicken or lamb, Indian food

Charcuterie Board: Aged cheddar, aged Gouda, goat cheese, spiced mixed nuts, pepperoni, Soppressata, raisins

Dessert: Lemon pound cake

Draft Cider

Level: Novice

Directions

Follow the basic recipe (page 58) with the following modifications:

1. Use sweet apples with low acidity. Most grocery store varieties meet this standard. See The Anatomy of Cider (page 72) for ideas.
2. Do not carbonate.
3. Do not add any extra sugars.
4. Keep the ABV below 6% (see Measuring ABV, starting on page 124).

Pairing Suggestions:

Entrée: Chinese, Indian, or other Asian takeout or homemade food

Charcuterie Board: Serrano ham, bacon, Camembert, apple slices (especially the same apples as fermented in your cider), wasabi peas, macadamia nuts, maple syrup

Dessert: Crème brûlée

Farmhouse Style/Scrumpy
Level: Advanced

Directions
Follow the base recipe with the following modifications:

1. Use crab apples or other more tannic varieties. See The Anatomy of Cider (page 72) for ideas.
2. Do not use any yeast.
3. Do not filter, clarify, or carbonate.

This cider relies on natural yeast, so you will not use any yeast other than that found on the apples. You'll need to pick, press, and juice these apples yourself, or ask for a local orchard to press them for you. The apples should be very ripe before pressing. The juice base cannot be pasteurized or have any additives, because they will kill the natural yeast. For this reason, you must use an orchard you trust to avoid using unsafe materials—apples that have been sitting for a long time or have more brown spots than normal. This recipe is best if you can grow and monitor the apples you use yourself.

Pairing Suggestions:

Entrée: Roasted pork chop with Granny Smith apples and onion sautéed with thyme and blue cheese sauce

Charcuterie Board: Manchego, aged cheddar, Brie, Marcona almonds, dried apricots, fig jam

Dessert: Sweet pastries; nothing bitter

French-Style or Cidre
Level: Very advanced
Equipment: 2 glass carboys
                    stopper with hole and airlock
                    food storage containers
                    funnel

siphon
bottler
bottles made for carbonated beverages
caps

Ingredients: 20 lbs tannic apples (sharps and bitters)
1 Campden tablet; crushed
1 packet champagne yeast

Directions

1. Sanitize food storage containers (including lids).
2. While food storage containers are soaking, wash and mill apples.
3. Place pulp in food storage containers and allow to sit for at least 24 hours. During this time the apples oxidize.
4. Press the juice out of the apples. Funnel juice and crushed Campden tablet into carboy topped with a stopper and airlock, and allow to settle in a cool, dark place. Check, starting at day 5.
5. You want a brown gel film to form at the top of the liquid. If the film is white you'll need to start over—white means fermentation was too early and quick.
6. On day 7, if you have a brown film, carefully siphon the clear liquid sitting between the brown top and sediment at the bottom into a sanitized carboy.
7. Add ¼ teaspoon of yeast and top carboy with a rubber stopper and airlock. Store for at least 30 days before bottling.

Note: This complex cider process is called "keeving"; there are many resources available on how to make this process easier.

Pairing Suggestions:

Entrée: Grilled chicken kebabs with honey, honey BBQ wings

Charcuterie Board: Roasted turkey, pancetta, dried cranberries, dried tart cherries, burrata, mascarpone, spiced nuts

Dessert: Cinnamon apple pie

Ice Cider

This style is rising in popularity, and while it takes a few extra steps and extra ingredients, you can make it at home and wow your friends. When pairing ice cider, avoid overly sweet dishes. Sweets will bring out the acid in the cider and kill the palate.

Follow the basic recipe (page 58) with the following modifications:

1. Freeze five gallons of fresh pressed apple juice or cider in a cleaned and sanitized PET carboy.
2. Slowly allow it to melt and separate the juice from the ice. Do this by placing the PET carboy over a sanitized barrel to collect the juice.
3. Ice cider is a difficult fermentation, so make sure to use yeast nutrient even if you usually skip it when making cider.

Pairing Suggestions:

Entrée:	Chicken cordon bleu, Monte Cristo sandwiches, bacon-wrapped dates
Charcuterie Board:	Blue cheese, sharp cheddar, aged Gouda, Brie, prosciutto, bacon, pears, raspberries
Dessert:	Cheesecake, lemon bars

Perry

Level: Novice

Follow the basic recipe (page 58) but replace half of the apple juice with pear juice.

Pairing Suggestions:

Entrée:	Scallops, fish and chips, tarragon roasted chicken
Charcuterie:	Cheshire, mild goat cheese, Stilton, roasted pork, apple, pear, quince paste, Marcona almonds, macadamia nuts
Dessert:	Apple or pear tart

Wood-Aged

Wait! Don't skip this! There is a great product on the market called the Oak Bottle that allows you to oak small amounts of wine. Consider purchasing one and aging some of your still cider in it. The result? A deliciously round, unusual cider like none anyone in your homebrew circle is making.

Pairing Suggestions:

Entrée: Lobster pot pie; caramelized onion, apple, and
                     Brie pizza
Charcuterie: Fontana, Brie, carrots, asparagus, mango,
                     dried apricot, bacon, white sausage
Dessert: Crème brûlée, butterscotch ice cream

Brew Cider, Improve the Earth— and Your Community

Want a reason to start brewing cider? Fruit trees are great for the environment.

Apple Trees and Air Quality

Apple and other fruit trees are excellent for the air. We learn from an early age that trees take in carbon dioxide, a harmful greenhouse gas, and release oxygen instead. In addition to carbon dioxide, trees also remove sulfur dioxide and carbon monoxide from the air we breathe.

Trees are responsible for evapotranspiration. Think of stepping out of the shower. You immediately feel cold, because when the water on your skin evaporates, it cools the air around you. That's evapotranspiration. This process, from one tree, can cool at the same level as ten room-size air conditioners in operation for twenty hours a day.

One tree can store thirteen pounds of carbon dioxide a year. That doesn't seem like much of an offset, but an orchard that is just one acre reduces carbon dioxide by 2.6 tons in just one year. That's how much carbon dioxide your car expends driving 26,000 miles—which is more than one trip around the earth if you drove along the equator.

Trees act as air filters, trapping dust, pollen, and smoke from the air. According to NC State University, dust in the air on the sheltered side of a tree can be as much as seventy-five percent lower than the unsheltered side.[12]

Fruit Trees Help beyond the Impact on Air

Orchards have natural mulch: fallen leaves protect the soil from the sun, lowering soil temperature and retaining moisture. The leaves

---

12 North Carolina State University College of Agriculture and Life Sciences Department of Horticulture. "Americans are planting . . . Trees of Strength." *https://projects.ncsu.edu/project/treesofstrength/ benefits.htm*. n.p. n.d. Web.

that fall to the ground and are dampened will rot, providing nutrition for organisms in the soil that continue to nourish the trees.[13]

We don't hear about it, but trees help keep our water supply cleaner. Storm water runoff can be a problem, but trees reduce surface water runoff from storms. This, in turn, limits soil erosion and reduces the amount of sediment in streams. Fruit trees increase ground water recharge, reducing the number of harmful chemicals deposited in streams.

Ground water recharge is the natural filtration process water goes through as it goes from the surface to the layers below near tree roots.

The Economy and Environmental Impact of Buying Local

Buying apples or cider from your local orchard allows you to support your local community. Local businesses recirculate

13 North Carolina State University College of Agriculture and Life Sciences Department of Horticulture. "Americans are planting . . . Trees of Strength." *https://projects.ncsu.edu/project/treesofstrength/ benefits.htm*. n.p. n.d. Web.

money into the local community.[14] A 2011 study found that spending one hundred dollars at an independently owned business results in fifty-eight dollars going into the local economy.[15] Spending the same amount at a nationally owned chain only yields thirty-three dollars for the local economy.

Local businesses employ locals who live, shop, and eat in the communities where they work, improving the local economy. Keep this in mind when picking out the apples you'll use in your cider.

If you've ever stopped at a farm stand or are a member of a CSA, you know that the closer you eat your food to when it was picked or killed, the better it tastes. What you may not realize is that there are other reasons to buy your food from local farms. Transportation in large trucks means massive emissions. Here in the Northeast of the United States, much of our produce at large grocery stores comes from California and Mexico. That's a lot of fossil fuels to get produce into the store. And it has been sitting for quite some time, which means it doesn't taste nearly as good as fresh. Buying apples for your cider from a local orchard or farm stand means you're getting better tasting, fresher produce, and significantly reducing carbon emissions.[16]

---

14   Institute for Local Self-Reliance. "Key Studies: Why Local Matters". *Ilsr.org/key-studies-why-local-matters/.* n.p. n.d. Web. 8 Jan. 2016.

15   "Going Local: Quantifying the Economic Impacts of Buying from Locally Owned Businesses in Portland, Maine." Garrett Martin and Amar Patel, *Maine Center for Economic Policy,* Dec. 2011.

16   SF Gate. "How Do Fruit Trees Help The Environment?" homeguides. sfgate.com/fruit-trees-environment-59135.html. n.p. n.d. Web.

The Anatomy of Cider

Craft cider is rising in popularity. In fact, of all the alcoholic beverage industries in the US, it grew the fastest from 2011 through 2016.[17] It's hard to know why, but there are definitely some good guesses out there. First, it's naturally gluten-free, which benefits the growing population of people sticking to a gluten-free diet. Additionally, cideries are getting creative by introducing flavors and hopping their ciders. Whatever the reason, more and more people are enjoying cider and more and more home brewers are making it at home.

While single varietal is cool on the label, the best ciders come from a blend of apples to balance three key qualities: sweetness, tartness, and bitterness. Aim for a 10:7:3 ratio of these characteristics to start and then play around to get your ideal blend.[18] You can pick your favorite apples from each qual-

---

17 To Market Magazine. "Craft Cider Is the Next Craft Beer." www.to marketmagazine.com/stories/2016/9/9/craft-cider-is-the-next-craft -beer. n.p. n.d. Web.

18 Peaceful Valley Farm Supply. "How to Make the Best Apple Cider." *www.groworganic.com/organic-gardening/articles/mix-apple-varieties- for-the-best-cider.* n.p. n.d. Web. 18 Oct. 2012.

ity or let the orchard use what they have. You'll end up with a great cider when you start with the 10:7:3 rule.

Sweet	Tart	Bitter
High sugar, low acid, low tannin	*Low sugar, high acid, low tannin*	*Low sugar, low acid, high tannin*
Easily found at the grocery store	*The acid keeps bacteria at bay and allows for aging*	*Gives an astringent quality*
The sugar in these apples means an ABV of 6–9%		*Balances sweetness*
Golden Delicious	Gravenstein	Dolgo Crabapple
Fuji	McIntosh	Cortland
Gala	Northern Spy	Newtown
Red Delicious	Winesap	Foxwhelp
Jonagold	Liberty	Porter's Perfection
Macoun	Rhode Island Greening	Chisel Jersey
Honeycrisp	Granny Smith	Somerset Redstreak
Porter's Perfection	Newtown Pippin	Harry Master's Jersey
Ashmead's Kernal	Baldwin	Dabinette
Golden Russet	Cortland	Brown Snout
Wickson Crab	Esopus Spitzenburg	Michelin
McIntosh	Golden Russet	Kingston Black
Virginia Crab	Wickson Crab	Virginia Crab[19]

19 Serious Eats. "Cider Apple Guide: Sharps, Sweets, and Sharp-Sweets." *drinks.seriouseats.com/2013/09/cider-apple-guide-american-varieties-sharp-sweet-delicious-gala-fuji-granny-smith-greening-jonathan-pippin-gravenstein.html.* n.p. n.d. Web.

Some of the apples appear in multiple columns because they have a complex flavor profile and combine traits of more than one category. Experiment with apples to find the perfect blend for your ideal tipple.[20]

20 Cider School. "What is a Cider Apple?" *www.ciderschool.com/orcharding/apples/.* n.p. n.d. Web.

10. Brewing Cider the Natural Way

MAKING CIDER USUALLY requires sweet, or nonalcoholic, cider and some yeast. But yeast exists naturally and is found on wild-growing apples. By picking apples yourself, and not buying them at the grocery store, you have everything you need to make cider. Before starting this process it's important to understand a few things about brewing cider naturally.

First, you'll have to crush and press the apples into cider yourself. Apple presses are not cheap, so I recommend trying to find a friend who already has the equipment. Check out local home brewing groups—you may have someone right in your neighborhood willing to let you borrow theirs in return for a small amount of homebrewed hard cider. This is a great way to meet other brewers in your area.

The second thing to remember is that batches of cider made from wild apples, or apples picked at an orchard, will vary significantly because of the types of yeast growing on them. Yeast comes in many hundreds of strains. Different yeasts prefer different temperatures and require different amounts of sugar, so it's impossible to predict whether you'll wind up with a drier or sweeter cider.

Finally, unless you cultivate the yeast from the cider, it is unlikely you will create the same batch again. I'll get into how to cultivate yeast later in this chapter.

Because this process uses freshly picked apples instead of pasteurized cider, there are risks. Do not use apples off the ground or any that appear rotten. Cut off any soft or brown spots before pressing the apples.

Still want to do it? Here's how.[21]

---

21   Grow Forage Cook Ferment. "How to Make Hard Cider with Wild Yeast." www
      .growforagecookferment.com/hard-cider-with-wild-yeast/. n.p. n.d. Web.

You'll Need:

- *Apples*. You'll pick these from the wild or an orchard. If you have crab apples on your property, use some in your mix to get the best balance. You cannot use store-bought apples because they are rinsed and waxed, meaning they will not have yeast on them and thus will not ferment.
- *A one-gallon, wide mouth container.* This should be glass.
- *A long, stainless steel spoon.* The spoon should be longer than the wide mouth container is tall.
- *A large piece of cheesecloth and rubber bands.*
- *A one-gallon glass carboy, rubber stopper and airlock, and siphon.*

While you can use plastic equipment, glass or steel work better.

The Process:

1. Clean and sanitize the wide mouth jar.
2. Rinse any dirt and leaves from the apples. Don't use any sort of vegetable or fruit wash on them.
3. Cut any rotten spots off the apples and then press and crush following the equipment's specifications.
4. Put the freshly squeezed cider in the wide mouth container. Leave between two and three inches at the top for when the cider starts to foam.
5. Fold the cheesecloth a few times into a square and place over the mouth of the jar. Secure with rubber bands.
6. Move the container to a dark place.
7. Daily remove the cheesecloth and stir with the long spoon. You'll want to make sure you clean and sanitize the spoon each day before stirring.
8. After two or three days you should notice some foam and activity in the jar. Once that happens, it's time to transfer.
9. Sanitize the carboy, rubber stopper and airlock, and siphon.
10. Use the siphon (whatever method you prefer) to transfer from the wide mouth jar to the carboy. Fit with the drilled bung and airlock.

11. Set the carboy in a dark place where it will not be disturbed or exposed to light.

12. Keep an eye on the airlock; when it stops bubbling (it should take about a week), go ahead and bottle.

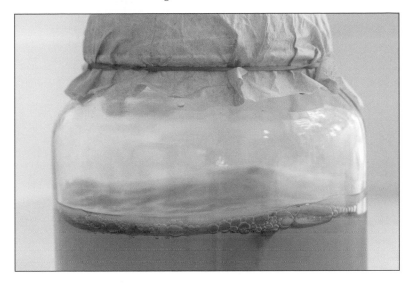

Cultivating Yeast

If you really like the flavor, you can cultivate the yeast to use later. After bottling, sanitize a small jar or food storage container with a fitted lid and a funnel. Funnel the dregs—the yeasty mush at the bottom of the carboy—into the newly sanitized container. You can keep this for eight to ten weeks in the fridge in your airtight container.

You can cultivate yeast in the wild, or right in your kitchen. One way is to simply work with the water you use to boil potatoes. This is an organic, natural way to cultivate yeast and move toward more sustainable, waste-minimal brewing. If you are going to boil potatoes and will use at least a cup and a half of water to do so, you can cultivate and grow yeast that can be used for brewing or baking.

You'll Need:
- A large jar and lid
- Funnel
- 1½ cups of the water the potatoes boiled in
- 1 cup whole wheat flour
- 1 Tbsp sugar

Process:
1. Sanitize the jar, lid, and funnel.
2. Allow the water to cool down and then funnel it into the sanitized glass jar.
3. Add the flour and sugar; stir until stiff.
4. Cover the mixture and store in a warm place overnight.
5. The next morning the mixture should be bubbling.

Once you have bubbling yeast, you should move it to the fridge. Every four days you'll need to feed the yeast. Take it from the fridge and set aside one cup. Replace the removed cup with a cup of water and cup of flour. Return container to the fridge and repeat this every four days.

The removed one cup can be dried and stored for use in baking bread. You'll need a sanitized cookie sheet. Spread the cup of removed yeast on the cookie sheet and place in an oven set at its lowest setting. You want the yeast to dry out but not cook—cooking it will kill the yeast, rendering it ineffective. Once it's dry, flake and store in an airtight storage container. You can store the dried yeast in either the fridge or freezer.

When you use the yeast you cultivated in home brewing, be sure to double or triple the amount the recipe calls for.

11. What Is Herbal Wine?

Herbal Wine: Can We Make This a Thing?

Herbal wine is a broad category of wine that includes wine not made from grapes or honey. It is also called worty wine. One well-known version is dandelion wine, but any non-poisonous plant can be fermented into wine. While mead and cider are seeing a rise in popularity among drinkers and home brewers, herbal wine hasn't caught on. Yet. This is surprising. In addition to its massive points for sustainability, which we'll get to in a few paragraphs, herbal wine is perfect for urban or limited space home brewers; you can make delicious herbal wine with less equipment than any other quick fermentable!

Herbal wine has its roots in ancient times and, like mead, was likely discovered accidentally. All that's needed to make it is plant matter, water, wild yeast, and time. While winemaking has focused on *vitis vinifera*, there are places where herbal wine has a rich history. There is probably no place where it is more beloved and part of the culture than Appalachia.

What's Appalachia? It's a region within the eastern US that isn't determined by any legal boundary but instead a cultural connection.[22] It is easy to associate Appalachia with the Appalachian Mountains, which stretch from Belle Isle in Canada to Cheaha Mountain in Alabama, but the region is smaller. It also should not be confused with the Appalachian Trail, the popular hiking trail that stretches from the base of Springer Mountain near Ellijay, Georgia, to the summit of Mount Katahdin in Northeast Piscataquis, Maine. The cultural region of Appalachia spans from the Southern Tier of New York State to northern Alabama, Mississippi, and Georgia.

The culture of Appalachia is one with roots in the land, a strong focus on practical skills, and a significant coal-mining population.

---

22 The Alliance for Appalachia. "What is Appalachia?" *thealliance forappala-chia.org/background/what-is-appalachia*. n.p. n.d. Web.

The region is not wealthy in the traditional sense, but has much to offer to its people and those who get to know it. There is a deep respect for the earth and quality goods that come from it.

This tie to the land has allowed residents to develop skills like canning and preserving and making moonshine and herbal wines!

Herbal Wine and Homesteading

Herbal wine is one of the easiest beverages to brew in a completely self-sustaining way. Any edible herb or plant can be turned into wine with the addition of commercial yeast, or with natural yeast that exists on the plant matter or is taken from other plants. It's also incredibly green. Plants that grow to excess, like herbs, can be used in tea and wine to avoid the compost pile.

Green Drinkers: Unite

Herbal wine is perfect for any home brewer who wants to live a more ethical life. That's because herbal wine, as mentioned, is sustainable. Anyone, whether they live in the middle of nowhere or in the center of a large city, can make herbal wine, thanks to foraging.

Foraging is the practice of picking ingredients that grow wild, rather than those cultivated in a garden. Foraging can be done while at the park, on your lunch break, hiking, or walking the dog. Before you go out and start picking, though, there are a few things to keep in mind. Always put safety first. Don't eat, cook, or brew with any plants you cannot identify confidently. If you're new, stick to basic items you know by sight. Believe it or not, you can forage plenty of things you've seen at the grocery store, if you know where to look. There are also many foraging clubs in local communities (check your local library and outdoor outfitters) that will teach you how to identify wild plants. The foraging community is always excited to bring new people in and happy to teach. Pretty soon you'll be expanding your knowledge of edible plants for winemaking and other purposes.

Also be aware of bees and wasps. Where there is sun-ripened fruit or any sort of flowers, there are also stinging insects, and while a sting or two is safe for most people, it's important to understand the risk of swarms of wasps. Make sure to pay attention to ground nests and avoid them at all times. In late autumn, wasps are especially aggressive. If you have a bee or wasp allergy, always carry epinephrine and any other prescribed medications, and don't go out alone.

You should only forage from wild plants. Never go onto private property or poach from a garden. Obey any posted signs.

Be mindful not to decimate a bush, shrub, tree, or vine, but instead be respectful of the plant's purpose as a source of food for other living beings and as an important part of the food chain. What makes herbal wine so forage-friendly, though, is that it can be made of a combination of ingredients, which means you don't need pounds and pounds of one ingredient. You can instead pick a little of this and a little of that. One-gallon batches of herbal wine require six to eight cups of herbs (more on this in the next chapter).

The Internet is a wonderful thing and one of the best resources for foragers of every level is the online map known as "Falling Fruit." Go to fallingfruit.org to access a worldwide, crowdsourced map that can be filtered to find whatever you're looking for. You can look near where you live or where you're going, or filter by the plants you're looking for. A typical search can be localized and open or specific (e.g., red raspberries in the Hudson Valley of New York). Orange circles with numbers appear and as you hone in on the location, pink dots appear. Clicking a dot brings up information about the area. This can include trailhead directions, good times to go, and tips to help you find particular yields. Additionally, users post notes when items are on private property owned by landowners willing to grant permission for foraging.

12. Making Your First Batch of Herbal Wine

HERBAL WINE—WHILE not as popular among home brewers as beer, cider, and mead—is the perfect quick fermentable. Free ingredients? Great! Only a few pieces of equipment? Sign me up. This book explores brewing one-gallon batches of herbal wine using a basic, quick recipe. There are plenty of steps that can be added later, like increased aging and carbonation, but to start you'll be enjoying these brews with very little work and far less time than most.

The equipment and ingredients that are needed are listed below. Because herbal wine appeals to homesteaders, zero waste households, and freegans, I've included additional information on building your setup using alternative items.

What You Need to Brew a One-Gallon Batch of Herbal Wine

Equipment:
- 2 one-gallon carboys (glass) and caps
- Airlock
- Drilled bung (rubber stopper)
- 2 stainless steel pots of at least 1.5 gallon capacity
- Cheesecloth or fine mesh sieve
- Funnel
- Small ladle

- Small drinking glass
- Racking can and auto siphon (or rubber tubing)
- Bottle wand
- Bottles
- Caps (unless using swing top bottles)
- Bottle capper

Ingredients:
- 1 gallon water
- 6–8 cups fresh herbs, destemmed
- 1 packet champagne yeast
- 2 lbs sugar
- ½ tsp yeast energizer (optional)
- 1 tsp yeast nutrient (optional; you can also use raisins or a squirt of lemon juice)

Process

This starter recipe is very basic and a great way to learn how to make a dry herbal wine. It does take a few days, so be sure to read the directions. Once you have a clean tasting batch, feel free to experiment with the other recipes in this book or those you find online. See the resources section of this book for great places to find recipes online. The first version of the directions is very detailed, so if you're an experienced home brewer, feel free to skip to the abbreviated, chart version that follows. Your wine is made from an herbal tea. There are a few steps involved in this process that take only a few minutes of hands-on work, but a few days of waiting. I recommend starting with mint wine to learn the process.

Day 1

1. *Boil the water.* Pour the gallon of water into your pot, cover it, and turn the heat on high. The water will get to a boil faster and you'll expend less energy if it is covered.
2. *Bruise the herbs.* While the water is heating up, lay the herbs on some wax paper or a smooth cutting board. Take a spoon (a

soup or large eating spoon is the best). Grasp the handle low
and set your thumb in the spoon. Roll it over the herbs. See
the section about destemming and bruising herbs (page 108)
for more information.

3. *Start the tea (sieve method).* When the water is boiling, turn
off the heat and drop the destemmed, bruised herbs into
the water. Put the cover back on the pot and allow to steep
for at least two days. They'll be strained out later with a
sieve, which is a lot quicker and easier than the cheesecloth
method, mentioned in the tips at the end of the chapter.

Day 3

1. *Acclimate your yeast.* Two to three hours before brewing, take
the yeast out of the fridge and set it on the counter to allow it
to warm up to room temperature.

2. *Clean and sanitize* the carboy, sieve, funnel, ladle, and small
drinking glass. If you're using a regular thermometer
(instead of a Fermometer), you'll need to clean and sanitize
that, too.

3. *Finish the tea (sieve method).* Strain the water and herbs
through a fine mesh sieve into your second pot.

4. *Boil.* Bring the tea to a boil and then remove from heat. Stir in
the sugar to make the wort.

5. *Cool and pitch your yeast.* Monitor the temperature of the wort;
when it is nearing 80°F, use the sanitized ladle to remove a
small amount of the wort and pour it into the small drinking
glass. Add the yeast to the sample. When the yeast starts to
work (you'll notice it fizz), use your funnel to pour it into the
cleaned, sanitized carboy. The yeast should begin to work in
about ten minutes. Use the funnel and pour the small sample
of wort and active yeast into the carboy. Add the rest of the
wort to the carboy using the funnel.

6. *Shake it up.* Use the cap that came with the carboy and cover it
tightly. Shake vigorously to oxygenate.

7. *Set aside.* Place the clean and sanitized drilled bung and airlock in the carboy and store in a stable temperature, dark environment for a month.

Day 33

1. Check the carboy and airlock. There should be a layer of yeast at the bottom and no more than one bubble per minute in the airlock. There also shouldn't be any movement in the wort. If there is still activity, wait another week and check again. Otherwise, move to step 2.
2. Clean and sanitize racking equipment. You'll clean and sanitize your second carboy, rubber tubing, and another drilled bung and airlock
3. Siphon from primary to secondary. Use the siphoning method you've practiced, and carefully, without introducing air, move your wort off the yeast from your primary to secondary fermenter. Cap with a clean drilled bung and airlock.
4. Wait again. Put your wort back in a place with a stable temperature away from the light.

Day 63

1. Check for activity. Check the airlock for bubbles. There shouldn't be any activity. If there is, you can leave it for another month or re-rack into a clean, sanitized carboy and then wait another month. If there is no activity, move to step 2.
2. Clean and sanitize your bottles, caps, and tubing for the bottling wand. You can also sanitize the bottle capper.
3. Fill and cap bottles. Use the bottling wand to fill your bottles and then cap them.

After you place the wine in bottles, let it age at least one month. When you open a bottle to drink, keep notes to see how aging affects it—this is how you'll find the sweet spot for future batches of the same recipe.

Tips

1. You can use a cheesecloth to make a tea bag for making the tea. Place the herbs in a piece of cheesecloth, gather the edges, and tie off. Soak when starting the process and then squeeze out all of the extra liquid instead of using a strainer.

2. If you use a balloon or piece of a balloon to replace an airlock, you should pierce it with a sanitized pin, a tack, or straightened paper clip. Place it over the opening. It will stand up as it works but should not inflate—doing so will end up ripping the latex. If your balloon starts to inflate, widen the hole a little using the sanitized pin.

3. You can bottle in wine bottles. Instead of recycling beer bottles and using caps, you can reuse wine bottles. Just as with caps, don't reuse corks unless they are made for that purpose. Sanitize wine bottles as you would caps.

Step	Equipment/ Ingredients	Why	Notes
Day 1			
BOIL	Stainless steel pot; 1 gallon water	Start the infusion	You do not need to sanitize the pot since you'll boil the water.
BRUISE HERBS	Spoon; Herbs	Release oils	
MAKE TEA	Herbs	Create wort	Set aside for 2 days.
Day 3			
ACCLIMATE YEAST	Yeast	Get it up to appropriate pitch temperature	If you forget to do this early, do it as soon as you remember.
PREP	Carboy, sieve, funnel, ladle, and small drinking glass. If you're using a regular	Avoid flaws and corruption	Follow all directions and be careful—sanitizer is nasty stuff.

	thermometer (instead of a Fermometer) you'll need to clean and sanitize that, too.		
BOIL THEN REMOVE	Pot; ⅔ gallons water	Need to pasteurize but don't want to lose too much to evaporation.	If you're using an electric stove move your pot off the burner.
COOL FOR ABOUT 15 MINUTES			
PLACE IN PRIMARY	Must, glass carboy	Your must is ready to move to its new home.	Use a cleaned, sanitized funnel.
COOL		Yeast needs the bath water to be just right.	This can take hours, so pop in a solid stopper or stopper with hole/ airlock and distract yourself.
PITCH YEAST	½ packet of yeast	Aerate your must first by shaking, pouring into something sanitized and back, etc.	
PRIMARY FERMENTATION		Wrap in a tee shirt or black garbage bag if your must will sit in direct sunlight for any time.	

Equipment Tweaks for Minimalist Home Herbal Winemaking

Replace the carboy with any one-gallon container. It can be a plastic milk gallon container or a juice jar or even a one-gallon capacity water bottle. You'll need the matching cap or cover in order to aerate the wort after pitching the yeast.

Replace the bung and airlock with a balloon that will fit (snugly) over the opening at the top of the container. If you are using a large mouth container, another option is to cut a circle from a balloon and stretch it over the top of the container, with rubber bands to secure it. Some people use plastic wrap, but it is very difficult to sanitize and, during a vigorous fermentation, can split. Splitting, unless you're there to observe it and quickly fix it, can let oxygen in and corrupt your wine.

You'll need a pin, thumbtack, or paper clip. You'll use this to poke a hole in the balloon so that it can release carbon dioxide during fermentation.

This setup is perfect for many people: those who just want to try out brewing, people who don't have the money to spend on a kit, and those who are trying to embrace a minimal-waste or waste-free lifestyle.

13. Herbal Wine Flavors and Recipes

MAKING HERBAL WINE is particularly fun because the end result rarely tastes like the starting ingredients. Herbal wine made from mint can taste like white wine. Fruit wines will often retain their flavor and flower wines keep the essence of their original taste, but the flavor of kitchen herbs is totally transformed when fermented. Herbal wine is also easy to make. Whether you forage, grow herbs in your garden, or grow them on your kitchen counter, you can make herbal wine year round.

Herbal wine can be made dry or sweet; the base recipe in the preceding chapter is for a drier wine. To make a dry wine, use champagne yeast. For a sweeter wine, use a slower yeast or one specifically labeled for sweet wines (or one for mead, if you can find it). Lalvin 47 is always a good choice for sweeter wine. The following recipes use single ingredients or blends. Using them as a base, you can experiment with endless combinations.

Cilantro Wine

Level:	Novice
Equipment:	2 pots
	Primary and secondary fermentation vessels
	Drilled bung
	Airlock
	Smooth cutting board
	Knife
	Soup spoon

Ingredients: 1 gallon water

6–8 cups fresh cilantro

1 packet champagne yeast

2 lbs sugar

Yeast energizer (optional)

Yeast nutrient (optional; you can also use raisins
      or a squirt of lemon juice)

Process:

1. Pour the gallon of water into a pot, cover it, and turn on the heat.
2. While the water heats, lay the herbs out on a smooth cutting board and bruise them using a soup spoon.
3. Once the water boils, remove from heat and add the bruised herbs. Cover again and allow to steep for at least two days.
4. After two days, remove the yeast from the fridge and set on the counter, allowing it to warm to room temperature.
5. Clean and sanitize a carboy, the carboy cap, bung, airlock, sieve, funnel, ladle, and small drinking glass. If you're using a regular thermometer instead of an adhesive thermometer, make sure to clean and sanitize that, too.

6. When your equipment is ready, strain the tea into the second pot to remove the herbs.

7. Boil the tea and then remove from heat. Stir in the sugar to make your wort. Ladle a small amount into a drinking glass or other small container.

8. Allow the wort to cool to 80°F. Add yeast to the wort in the drinking glass. Wait until it's working (about ten minutes; you'll know when it's foaming or fizzing) and then funnel into the carboy. Funnel the rest of the wort into the carboy over the yeast mixture.

9. Place the sanitized carboy cap on the carboy and give everything a really good shake to oxygenate.

10. Remove the cap and replace with the drilled bung and airlock. Place in a stable environment safe from light for thirty days. Some herbal wines are done fermenting in the primary very quickly, as soon as five days. Feel free to check early, and if fermentation has gotten so slow that you've got fewer than one bubble a minute, go ahead and rack to secondary.

11. Check for fermentation. If bubbles appear in the airlock at a rate of more than one per minute, wait a few more days. Otherwise, clean and sanitize a second carboy, drilled bung and airlock, and the equipment you will use to rack from primary to secondary.

12. Allow your herbal wine to sit for thirty to sixty days in secondary before bottling.

13. Allow the bottled wine to age at least three months before tasting.

14. Don't forget to keep tasting notes so that you can drink future batches at their best.

Basil Wine

Basil wine requires a bit of trial and error. The result, according to expert herbal winemaker Jack Keller, should be rich, spicy, and peppery, with hints of mint and clove.

Level: Novice

Equipment: 2 pots

Primary and secondary fermentation vessels

Drilled bung

Airlock

Smooth cutting board

Knife

Soup spoon

Ingredients: 1 gallon water

3-4 cups of fresh basil

1 packet champagne yeast

2 lbs sugar

Yeast energizer (optional)

Yeast nutrient (optional; you can also use raisins
or a squirt of lemon juice)

Process:

1. Boil the water, covered.
2. While the water heats, bruise the basil leaves and stems. Basil is a soft-stemmed plant and doesn't require destemming. It's

also incredibly flavorful, which means you can try skipping the bruising step if you find your basil wines come out too strong. Another option is to bruise some of the basil but not all of it.

3. Remove the boiling water from the heat and add the basil. Allow to steep for two days.

4. After two days, remove the yeast from the fridge and set on the counter, allowing it to warm. Remember, you don't want to shock your yeast, so allow it to warm up for two to three hours.

5. Clean and sanitize a carboy, the carboy cap, bung, airlock, sieve, funnel, ladle, and small drinking glass. If you're using a regular thermometer instead of an adhesive thermometer, make sure to clean and sanitize that, too.

6. Strain the tea and then bring to a boil.

7. Remove the tea from the heat and stir in the sugar. Remove some wort to a small, sanitized drinking glass and add yeast when it's about 80°F.

8. Let the yeast start working. This takes about ten minutes. The yeast is working when you notice bubbles or foam appearing.

9. Funnel the small sample of active yeast and wort into the carboy. Funnel the rest of the wort into the carboy over the yeast mixture.

10. Cover the carboy with its cap and shake it up to oxygenate.

11. Remove the cap and replace with the drilled bung and airlock. Place in a stable, dark environment and monitor. Check your airlock and once primary fermentation slows, rack to secondary. Your wine is ready to be transferred when bubbles appear at a rate of fewer than one per minute.

12. Because basil wine takes a while, consider racking every month for three months before bottling.

13. After bottling the wine, allow it to age at least three months before trying.

14. Keep good notes on tasting. Once you get your basil wine
right, you'll want to make more to share and enjoy with
friends. Good notes will help you figure out the perfect time
to drink it.

Parsley Wine

Level:	Novice
Equipment:	2 pots
	Primary and secondary fermentation vessels
	Drilled bung
	Airlock
	Smooth cutting board
	Knife
	Soup spoon
Ingredients:	1 gallon water
	6—8 cups fresh parsley, bruised
	1 packet champagne yeast

2 lbs sugar

Yeast energizer (optional)

Yeast nutrient (optional; you can also use raisins or a
squirt of lemon juice)

Process:

1. Boil the water, covered. While it heats, lay out and bruise the
   parsley using a soup spoon, flat edge of a knife, or kitchen
   mallet.
2. Once the water is boiling and the parsley is sufficiently
   bruised, remove the pot of water from the heat and add the
   parsley. Cover and allow the tea to steep for at least two days.
3. On brewing day, remove the yeast from the fridge and allow
   it to warm up for two to three hours to avoid shocking it when
   pitching. Clean and sanitize the equipment while the yeast is
   warming up to room temperature.
4. Strain the tea into a pot, squeezing to get as much of it as
   possible.
5. Boil the tea and then remove from heat. Stir in the sugar,
   making sure it dissolves completely. Ladle some into a small
   glass or other container.
6. Monitor the temperature of the small glass (it will cool faster
   than the large pot of tea) and when it reaches 80°F, add the
   yeast. It will take no more than ten minutes to start working.
7. Funnel the large pot of wort into the carboy and then pitch
   the active yeast and wort into the carboy.
8. Cap the carboy and give it several vigorous shakes to give the
   yeast some oxygen.
9. Replace the cap with the drilled bung and airlock. Place in
   a dark location where it will not experience temperature
   changes or exposure to light.
10. Check fermentation activity after five days. Once
    fermentation has slowed to fewer than one bubble per
    minute, rack to secondary. Use a drilled bung and airlock.

Wait thirty to sixty days before bottling. If there is a lot of sediment after thirty days, re-rack to avoid flaws in the final product.

11. Bottle and allow to age at least three months.

12. Keep tasting notes for future batches.

Beet Wine²³

Although not herbs, beets make a delicious wine worthy of inclusion here. Beets have more sugar than many other vegetables but are high in fiber, potassium, folate, iron, and other nutrients. Beet wine also creates very little waste, since the beets are boiled to make the tea but then can be eaten or used in other recipes. Another great thing about this recipe is that the tea doesn't require steeping—you can get from prep to primary in one day.

Level: Intermediate

Equipment: 2 pots

---

23 Beet Wine Recipes. "The Winemaking Home Page." *http://winemaking.jack-keller.net/recipe2.asp* n.p. n.d. Web. 27 Sep. 2007. (Modified from Jack Keller's recipe which is cited as being C.J.J. Berry's *First Steps in Winemaking*.)

Primary and secondary fermentation vessels

Drilled bung

Airlock

Smooth cutting board

Knife

Soup spoon

Ingredients: 1 packet champagne yeast

1 lemon, zested and juiced

6 whole cloves

½ oz shredded ginger

1 gallon water, divided

3 lbs beets

3 lbs sugar

Yeast energizer (optional)

Yeast nutrient (optional; you can also use a raisins or a squirt of lemon juice)

Process:

1. Remove the yeast from your fridge and set out to allow it to acclimate to room temperature (about two to three hours).
2. Funnel the lemon juice, cloves, ginger, and half of the water into your carboy.
3. Wash the unpeeled beets very well and dice into ¼-inch cubes.
4. Place diced beets and lemon zest in a pot with the rest of the water and bring to a boil, cooking until the beets are tender. Do not overcook—the beets should be tender, not mushy.
5. When the beets are done, add the sugar and stir until completely dissolved. Strain into funnel into the primary fermentation vessel, saving a little in a small glass. Cap and shake the carboy to oxygenate the yeast. (Cooked beets can be eaten or used in soups, etc.)
6. When the reserved wort cools to between 75 to 80°F, add the room temperature yeast. If you're using yeast energizer and nutrient, add it now.

7. Fit the carboy with a drilled bung and airlock. Move carboy to a setting where it will not receive light and where the temperature will remain stable at the warm end of room temperature. Give it a swirl every day for three days.

8. On the third day, strain into secondary vessel and fit with a drilled bung and airlock.

9. Monitor regularly. When bubbles reduce to less than one per minute and wort is clear, rack and bottle.

10. Allow to bottle-age for at least one year.

According to Jack Keller, this recipe yields a medium-bodied beet wine. If you want a higher-bodied version, increase the beets to four pounds and reduce the sugar used to two.

Blackberry Wine[24]

24 Blackberry Wine Recipes. "The Winemaking Home Page." *http://winemaking.jackkeller.net/recipe2.asp* n.p. n.d. Web. 27 Sep. 2007. (Modified from Jack Keller's recipe which is cited as adapted from C.J.J. Berry's 13 New Winemaking Recipes.)

Whether you decide to go foraging for wild blackberries, have your own cultivated bushes, or get them at the farmers' market, you can't go wrong with blackberry wine. It will taste like blackberries but remind you of Merlot. Play with aging, yeast, and the amount of fruit and sugar—the possibilities are endless.

Level: Advanced

Equipment: Pots
Primary and secondary fermentation vessels
Drilled bung
Airlock
Bowl
Fine metal sieve
Small bottle
Balloon
Pin, tack, or straightened paper clip

Ingredients: 1 packet champagne yeast
1 gallon water
4 lbs fresh, ripe blackberries
3 lbs sugar
Yeast nutrient and energizer (optional)

Process:

1. Remove yeast from the fridge so that it can sit out for two to three hours before pitching. Once it has acclimated to room temperature, pitch it in a small amount of water according to the directions on the packet.
2. While the yeast is warming up, start boiling the water.
3. Wash and drain the berries well; shaking them in the colander and washing in batches helps with the removal of excess water. Crush them in a bowl and then transfer to carboy.
4. Funnel the gallon of boiling water into the carboy and mix well.

5. When the mixture is cooled to about 75°F, pitch the active yeast.

6. Fit the carboy with a drilled bung and airlock and set aside for four to five days. Swirl daily. The carboy should be left in a place that is on the warm side of room temperature (70 to 75°F) and away from the light.

7. Add the sugar to the secondary fermentation vessel. Strain the blackberry water through a fine mesh strainer onto the sugar in the secondary. Tap off to the shoulder, the place where the carboy starts to narrow. Reserve the extra. Fit with a drilled bung and airlock.

8. Wrap the carboy with t-shirts or sheets—this wine is very sensitive to light.

9. Take the excess from the primary and place in the small bottle. Pierce the balloon and fit it over the top.

10. Once fermentation has ceased (about a week), add the excess liquor to the larger batch and place in a cool (60 to 65°F), dark place for three months before racking.

11. Allow to sit for another two months, then rack and bottle.

12. Allow to sit for at least six months but up to a year for best flavor.

13. As always, keep notes on your process and the way the wine tastes at different times.

Ginger Wine[25]

Ingredients:
1 gallon water, divided
5–6 inches fresh ginger, peeled and grated
Sliced orange, including the peel and pith

---

25 Pixie's Pocket. "Ginger Wine: One Gallon Recipe." *http://www.pixiespocket. com/2017/10/ginger-wine.html.* n.p. n.d. Web.

4 cups sugar
1 packet champagne yeast
Yeast energizer and nutrient (optional)

Process:

1. Boil one quart of the water.
2. Add the ginger to the water.
3. Add the orange slices, including pith and peel, to the water. Stir, and lower the temperature. Simmer, covered, for at least an hour, adding more water if it loses too much.
4. Strain the tea and return it to the pot.
5. Add the sugar to the hot tea and stir until completely dissolved. Reserve a small amount. Cover the pot and allow wort to cool.
6. When the reserved wort reaches about 80°F add the yeast and allow it to start working. It should take no more than ten minutes.
7. Funnel the large batch of tea into the carboy. If there isn't enough to reach the shoulder of the carboy, top it off with water.
8. When it cools to 80°F, add the activated yeast. Top with a drilled bung and airlock. Store in a stable, warm place where it is out of the light.

9. When fermentation slows to fewer than one bubble per minute, rack to secondary and allow to finish fermentation and clear.

10. Bottle when clear and you have airlock bubbles appearing at a rate of less than 1 per minute. Bottle-age for at least three months.

Rose Petal Wine

Apply this recipe to any edible flower or blossom; just be sure to remove any green parts.

Ingredients: 6 cups rose petals, pinched at the bottom to avoid vegetal strike
¼ cup golden raisins
1 gallon water
4 cups sugar
Champagne yeast
Yeast energizer and nutrient (optional)

Process:

1. Bruise the petals and place in a pot with the raisins.
2. In a second pot, add about two thirds of the water and bring it to a vigorous boil.
3. Remove the water from the heat and stir in the sugar, continuing to stir until completely dissolved. Then pour into the other pot, over the rose petals. Allow to steep for two hours.
4. Once steeped, remove some of the wort and when it reaches 80°F, add about two thirds of the yeast in the packet. While waiting for the yeast to activate, strain the petal tea into a funnel and the carboy. Top it with the cap or a drilled bung and airlock.
5. When the mixture in the carboy reaches about 80°F, pitch the active yeast. Top with a drilled bung and airlock. Wrap the carboy in tee shirts or a sheet and set in a warm, stable place out of the light.
6. Allow to ferment from five to thirty days, making sure that activity in the airlock has reduced to no more than one bubble per minute. Then rack to secondary and allow to sit another thirty to sixty days before bottling.
7. Bottle-age for one to three months before enjoying.

Destemming and Bruising Your Herbs

It sounds like a mean thing to do, but your herbal wine will not reach its flavor potential if you don't destem and bruise your herbs. We're going to look specifically at cooking herbs, but I'll also show you how the same principles apply to all herbs. To keep things simple, I'm going to refer to rosemary, an herb most people are familiar with. Rosemary sprigs look a lot like pine tree branches and are, in fact, an evergreen plant. They have a woody stem and the fragrant needles that are the part we cook with. When you buy dried rosemary, it's the needles that are in the bottle. It's in these needles that you find the true essence of rosemary.

Found in every cell of every needle are oils that give rosemary its distinct flavor and aroma. These oils are not found in the stem, which is fairly bitter if you bite it. The needles smell great on their own, but become more pungent when bitten. That's because biting the needles ruptures cells, releasing the oils and exposing your tongue to them.

When cooking, it's not uncommon to chop herbs. This does a few things. First, it increases the surface area coming into contact with your food, thus spreading the flavor. Second, a large needle of rosemary can be uncomfortable to eat, even when cooked, because it is a firm needle that can be a bit sharp. Finally, when cooking herbs, smaller pieces will break down much more quickly.

Making wine is a little different. The herbs are only used to make a tea that forms the base of your wine. Thus a great deal of flavor must be imparted from the needles. There are two tricks to making sure that the tea is as flavorful as possible.

Before making the tea, destemming is crucial for herbs like rosemary that have a woody, twig-like stem. Leaving the stems in the tea can result in a bitter flavor because of the compounds found on and in those cells, and there may be an astringent feel from the tannins. There are also tannins in the needles, but it's a low enough amount that it actually helps the wine, while the stems can overload the tea. The stems also don't have the same oils, so you'll mask the flavor of the rosemary.

Herbs that have a woody stem (lavender, marjoram, mint varieties, oregano, rosemary, sage, thyme) are easy to destem. Simply grasp the stem in one hand at the top (the leaves/needles should be pointed toward this end) and pinch the stem with the fingers of the other hand just below. Pull the stem so that the leaves or needles pop off as the stem moves through the pinched fingers.

Some herbs have soft stems, like basil, cilantro, parsley, and tarragon. These do not need to be destemmed—their tender stems will not add any off flavors. If you do want to destem these anyway, you can pinch off the leaves with your thumbnail, but it's time consuming. Some people also use a knife to pull along the leaves, removing them from the stem.

In order to make your tea as flavorful as possible, bruising the herbs is the way to go (after destemming). Imagine a

rosemary needle. Chopping it ruptures cells along the cut edge, releasing the flavorful, aromatic oils. But there's a lot more in there. This is where bruising comes in. The idea is to crush as many cells as possible, increasing the amount of oils released. There are a few different methods that can be employed to bruise herbs.

Use a spoon. Lay the herbs on a smooth cutting board in a single layer. Grasp a spoon near the bottom of the handle and place your thumb in the inside curve of the spoon. Roll the outside curve over the herbs while applying pressure with your thumb. This rolling motion will bruise any herb, releasing oils onto the surface.

Use a knife or mallet. Another option is to lay the herbs on a smooth cutting board in a single layer and then press with the flat edge of the knife or a kitchen mallet.

Why use a smooth cutting board? I like to save a little of my boiling water and pour it over the herbs that are stuck to it, so that the very hot water collects any stuck herbs and the oils that have collected on it.

14. Describing Your Brews

WE ALL HAVE that friend who is a picky eater or drinker. Maybe they don't like certain spices, hoppy beers, or sweet wine. Your being able to sum up your rosemary wine or spiced mead in a few key terms will help picky people decide whether they're willing to try it.

It's not just the picky folk you'll use this language with, though. Maybe you brew a mead that's not quite "there," but you're not quite sure where "there" is. Being able to identify and name a few different tastes, and, possibly more importantly, "feels," will enable you to talk to more experienced brewers in person and online to bring your recipes to exactly where you want them.

By "feels" I don't mean the emotions your brews invoke (although drink enough of them and they will!). Much of what we experience when drinking, and what we seek out in favorite brews, is related to mouth feel. A drink can taste great but still be missing something. It's these descriptors that are hardest to pin down, but once you do you'll be on your way to brew-tasting like a pro.

The Four Basic Starter Terms

There are four basic terms that will help you describe your brews—both how they taste and how you want them to taste—to any home brewer or aficionado.

Sweetness and Dryness

Imagine sweetness and dryness on either end of a spectrum. The sweeter a brew is, the less dry. The dryer it is, the less you'd describe it as sweet. Acidity is often mistaken for dryness and is what makes a drink tart. A drink can be both sweet and feel tart (think of Sour Patch Kids) through residual sugars, but for the purposes of description we'll focus strictly on the mouth feel and not on the science.

Sweetness

A sweet brew will feel softer in your mouth. It may even feel oily on the middle and back of your tongue. Think of when you drink fruit punch or another sugary drink. If you want to get a sense of what sweetness does to your mouth, just grab a glass of water, an empty glass, and some simple syrup. Simple syrup is a solution of white sugar and water. Make it by dissolving three parts sugar in two parts warm water (do it on the stove, but don't let the water boil). Don't use artificial sweetener; it won't give you the same results.

Take a sip of plain water and swish it around your mouth. Next, put some water in the second glass and add a little simple syrup. Take some water in your mouth and swish it around. Note the differences in how the water feels in your mouth. Try to focus on the amount of sugar and how increasing sugar changes the feel in your mouth. You can experiment as much as you want. Watching calories? Just spit the water into a designated spit bucket and taste to your heart's content. If you're worried that you're losing sensitivity, sipping a little seltzer will refresh your palate.

Acidity

An acidic drink will make your mouth water, like when you bite into a Granny Smith or other tart apple. If it's very dry, your mouth will pucker, especially behind your lips. Think of when you eat a tart candy like Sour Patch Kids. That drying feeling is caused by acidity.

To feel acidity in your mouth you can do a similar tasting exercise to the one described above for sweetness. Get two glasses, some water, and a lemon or lemon juice. Fill one glass with water. In the other put water and add a little lemon juice. Notice how your mouth dries out as you drink and where you feel this in your mouth and throat. Pay special attention to the finish: the time after you swallow. Does it last longer as you increase the lemon juice?

The next two tasting descriptors are not related to each other. Like the first, though, they are more about the feel of the alcohol than the taste. Isn't it strange how these influence our enjoyment? Sweetness and acidity are easy to start with because we experience them in a lot of what we drink anyway. The next two, alcohol and astringency, are trickier to nail down because some of us never drink things that are astringent or are particularly high in alcohol. Check out the descriptions and then try the exercises to develop your sense of these. For alcohol, you will need to use actual alcohol to practice. Always be safe when consuming alcohol. I recommend spitting during the exercise so that you stay sharp.

Alcohol

The higher the ABV, the more alcohol your brew has. Some people like a more alcoholic brew and others like a drink where the alcohol is less pronounced. How do you know? Whether or not you measure ABV, you can assess how much alcohol you like in your drink based on the mouth feel.

Alcohol makes a drink bolder and adds heat. Your tongue will feel similar to when you eat spicy food. You'll also feel the alcohol at the back of your throat when you swallow. The finish will lengthen and leave your mouth, tongue, and throat with a hot feeling.

To experience varying levels of alcohol, you'll need two glasses, some water, and some vodka. Start, as always, by taking some water in your mouth and swishing it around, then spitting it out. Pour water into the second glass and add a little vodka. Take some in your mouth and swish. Add a little bit of vodka at a time to see how the increased ABV feels in your mouth, on your tongue, and in your throat. Be sure to take it easy with this one and consider spitting between tastes to stay at your sharpest.

Astringency

Astringency is the trickiest quality to define for new tasters. Dryness and astringency can go hand in hand and astringency also often brings bitterness, which makes it hard to identify. But astringency is a specific feel. You'll feel it with your tongue when you run it along the roof of your mouth. When you drink something astringent, the inside of your mouth and tongue will feel gravelly or sandpapery.

This tasting experience takes a little setup, but will have you identifying astringency like a pro in no time. For this tasting experience you'll need:

- 2 empty glasses (must be able to stand heat, don't use thin wine glasses)
- 1 tea cup or mug
- boiling water
- 1 tea bag with black tea

Instructions:

1. Place the teabag in a mug or teacup.
2. Place the empty glasses next to each other in a line (left to right).

3. Boil enough water to make one regular cup of tea (four to eight ounces).

4. Pour the water over the teabag.

5. After one minute, pour an ounce of the tea into the first (leftmost) glass. You can use a spoon or turkey baster to avoid spilling too much.

6. At the five-minute mark, pour an ounce of the tea into the second glass.

7. At ten minutes, remove the tea bag and place the mug in the rightmost position.

Take some of the tea from the one-minute sample and swish it around your mouth, paying attention to how your tongue experiences the roof of your mouth and inside of your cheeks. You can rinse your mouth with water or seltzer, and continue sampling. Each sample is increasingly astringent, giving you a sense of what you like and don't like when it comes to astringency.

Other Tasting Descriptors to Know

While these four are the basics, there are some other terms that will help you when describing your brews, especially as you become more experienced. Many of these refer to the main four and will be easy for you to identify once you master those. What follows are the forty-five most helpful terms for describing taste and feel.

Big: When someone refers to a drink as "big," they mean that it is highly alcoholic or very flavorful. One of these is pronounced. This is not a bad thing.

Biscuity/Bready/Yeasty: These three terms all mean that the yeast has influenced the flavor of the brew. In mead and some ciders, this may be desired. Leaving wort on the yeast longer can increase this flavor, whereas getting it off the yeast more quickly can reduce this flavor. In dry meads and ciders this can be an especially delightful flavor and feel.

Body: The weight of the drink in your mouth. The easiest way to think about body is to compare types of milk. Skim milk is the lightest bodied while whole milk is the heaviest. Practice noting the heft of each of these to start applying the same idea to alcoholic beverages.

Boozy: An overwhelming flavor or aroma of alcohol; usually used as a negative descriptor, as in the alcohol is out of balance and overwhelming the other aspects of the drink.

Brackish/Briny: Having mild saltiness in the flavor. Can be especially interesting and balance some brews, but can also detract from the flavor or come across as incongruous with the rest of the flavors.

Clean: This is a descriptor you want to hear. It doesn't mean "soapy," which is not a good quality in any brew. It means that the taste is flavorful and enjoyable without any off flavors. Not sure what off flavors are? Check out the section on troubleshooting your brews. Brews with off flavors are referred to as dirty. Dirty should not be confused with earthy.

Complex: Having a variety of aromas or flavors. This is a desirable quality. Think of a wine that is smoky or leathery in addition to having fruit aromas like plum or strawberry. Complexity comes from a clean brewing process and allowing a brew to age.

Crisp: Refers to a good amount of dryness in the mouth feel. Especially useful in describing cider.

Delicate: Light in the mouth. Can refer to flavor or body but is usually an overall descriptor. A rose petal herbal wine, for example, might be delicate.

Dirty: Used to describe a brew with evidence of flaws. The opposite of clean. Don't confuse dirty with earthy, which can be a desirable quality.

Earthy: With flavors or aromas of dirt, wood, or stone. This is desirable in some brews.

Flat: When referring to carbonated brews it means it's lost the carbonation, which is not a good thing. "Flat" may also refer to a lack of flavor.

Floral: Having an aroma of blossoms without being specific to one type of flower. Sometimes "perfumy" is used.

Fruity: Having the aroma or flavor of fruit. It can be followed with specifics (red berries or green apple) or used generally.

Full-bodied: Heavy on the tongue and in the mouth. The brew has heft.

Green: Referring to a brew that has not aged long enough and tastes young. Not the same as hollow.

Hazy: Not clear. This is desired in unfiltered brews. Haziness is not a flaw except in some competitions where extra points are given for clarity (generally points are not deducted for haze).

Heavy: A brew that is full-bodied and alcoholic is referred to as heavy. Great for winter brews.

Hollow: Missing something, lacking in flavor, acidity, or an unknown quality—leaves the drinker with a sense that the brew is incomplete. Different from green, where the thing that is missing is aging time.

Hot: Too alcoholic so that the brew leaves an unpleasant feeling on the tongue or in the back of the throat.

Husky: Very astringent, to the point of the tongue feeling pebbly as it runs along the roof of the mouth or insides of the cheeks.

Intense: Used to describe a strong flavor, aroma, or alcohol level.

Jammy: A strong, sweet, fruit flavor.

Medicinal: Tasting of chemicals or a flavor similar to cough syrup.

Metallic: This is an off taste that some people have trouble defining. If you've ever stuck your finger in your mouth after cutting it, blood tastes metallic. Also the weird way your hands smell after touching coins with wet hands.

Moldy/Musty/Mildewy: If a brew has these aromas or flavors, something went wrong in the process. This is never desirable.

Oaky: If your brew has odors of vanilla or wood or toasty flavors, it will often be referred to as oaky. That's because when alcohol is aged in oak barrels it gains these flavors.

Perfumy: Having floral aromas.

Peppery: Tasting of black pepper. Great in a winter brew and especially interesting with berry brews.

Powerful: Strongly alcoholic. Sometimes it's desirable, but without the right balance it can simply come off as hot.

Resinous: Piney or menthol flavor. Having a quality similar to eucalyptus.

Rich: High in flavor in a good way. Requires balance among other qualities.

Robust: A brew will be described as robust when it is in balance but everything about it is bold: aroma, alcohol, and mouth feel.

Round: Well-balanced.

Sharp: A strong presence of acid that is distracting.

Skunky: Sulphury. Think about a beer that has been exposed to the light or has been in an environment where it experienced big swings in temperature.

Smooth/silky: A soft mouth feel often found in sweeter, lower alcohol brews.

Sticky: Too sweet, especially when out of balance with other flavors. Can also describe a mouth feel that is unpleasantly oily.

Syrupy: Can refer to a brew that is very full-bodied or an overly sweet brew.

Tart: A positive descriptor describing a nice amount of sour flavors in a brew.

Texture: Another way to say "mouth feel."

Thick/Thin: Another way of saying full- or light-bodied.

Vegetal: Often found in green brews, this is a strike of flavor or aroma reminiscent of celery or other greenery.

Viscous: Thick and heavy mouth feel or body.

Watery: Too thin, tasting or feeling diluted. Light-bodied brews can be desirable but watery is a bad quality.

Young: Green; not aged long enough.

While you don't have to learn all of these terms, they will help you as you discuss different drinks you're tasting.

15. Troubleshooting Your Brews

WHAT THE FUNK? It happens to the best of us. Even when we sanitize and take every possible precaution, sometimes we get a batch that is downright funky. Sometimes it's just slightly funky. Sometimes it's funky but it's our new favorite thing. The official name for flavors that shouldn't be there are "faults." Here are some common off flavors and their common causes, as well as suggestions for combating them. Always remember: brewing is mostly trial and error.

Common Off Flavors[26]

Vinegary. This is caused by acetic acid. It sometimes comes from oxidation. Mead that seems to darken or brown early in the process is often a victim of oxidation. Wild yeast can also cause a sour taste, so consider changing that up. Sometimes mead tastes sour early in the process. If this improves with age, just keep aging. It's just not ready yet. Another reason can be fruit additions.

Tart. This comes from a low pH and can come from the acid level in honey, or bacteria due to a lack of proper cleaning and sanitizing.

Alcoholic. Yes, you want your mead to have alcohol, but if it's tasting too alcoholic you may have fermented at too high of a temperature. Your mead could just need to age longer. There could also be an issue with your yeast.

---

26 Beer Judge Certification Program. "Beer Faults." *https://www.bjcp.org/faults. php.* n.p. n.d. Web.

Wet newspaper. Anything that tastes like paper or cardboard is a sign of oxidation and, likely, a batch you'll need to dump. To avoid this, be really careful about introducing oxygen after fermentation. Practice siphoning with water—siphoning errors are the most common culprit in oxidation. If you're using swing top bottles, check the seal. Store your mead in a cooler place.

Chemical tastes. Usually this is a balancing issue. Add less nutrient or fewer excess ingredients like yeast energizer and nutrient.

Cloying. This refers to sweetness or flabbiness (a lack of structure). Try using less honey and consider adding a balancing acid or even tannin. You can usually fix this flaw rather than dumping the whole batch.

Fruity (strawberry, pear, banana, grape, citrus). Usually a sign of yeast stress. Can happen if must isn't oxygenated enough or if not enough yeast was pitched. Bottle conditioning and longer aging might help.

Metallic. This is often an issue with your water, but check your equipment for rust, too. Experiment with your cleaning/sanitizing process. You can send your water for analysis to get a profile. This helps novice brewers learn their water so they can adjust it with salts.

Moldy. This is another taste that signifies oxidation. Check your cleaning/sanitizing procedure and check water. Make sure all ingredients are fresh.

Band-aid. Sounds crazy, but you'll know this one as soon as you taste it. It's from phenol or carbonic acid and it's an infection that means it's time to dump your batch. Your yeast may not be healthy. This can also present as a medicinal taste.

Nutty. Yet another indicator that your mead has been oxidized.

Solvent. It burns! A burning sensation on the palate is sometimes referred to as "solvent" and is most likely a yeast issue. It can happen from fermenting at too high a temperature or from yeast that isn't fresh.

Sulphur. Mead left on the yeast for too long between rackings at too high of a cellaring temperature can experience yeast autolysis, resulting in rotten egg flavor. This can also happen if the water used has a high level of sulfates.

Tannic. Tannins are present on common additions like raw spices and fruit peels and pith. Rinse well or use those that aren't too tannic. If you added tannins to your brew because you wanted some astringency, just reduce the amount you use next time.

Green. This is also referred to as vegetal. Sometimes it smells like canned or rotten cabbage, celery, onion, asparagus, or parsley. Results from weak yeast or slow fermentation. Can also result from stale ingredients or equipment that was not properly sanitized.

Waxy. Yet another result of oxidation or a problem with your honey. Try filtering or using a different variety of honey.

Yeasty. This is one of the easiest flaws to spot and diagnose since you know what yeast tastes like. A mead struggling with this can also taste like bread. This can be a simple issue of siphoning too low and grabbing yeast cake or not giving the yeast enough time. This can be fixed by adding a clarifier.

Oxygen: Aeration vs. Oxidation

The most common culprit causing your brews to fail? Oxygen. The tricky thing about oxygen is that early in the process, it's good. You add oxygen to your must, or wort, before adding yeast. This process is called aeration. Yeast needs oxygen to grow and reproduce, so pumping your must with oxygen gets your brew started off on the right foot.

After fermentation starts, however, the introduction of oxygen should be avoided. This later introduction of oxygen can produce byproducts like dactyl, which can give your brews a sweet, butterscotch flavor. Do what you can to avoid any introduction of oxygen once fermentation begins.

One of the most common ways oxygen is introduced is by splashing. Be very careful when moving, racking, and bottling or kegging that you do so smoothly. I can't stress enough the importance of practicing whatever siphon method you choose so that you can siphon without letting any oxygen sneak in.

Yeast: Friend and Foe

The faults that arise from problems with yeast can often be avoided by taking care to use healthy, active yeast at the right temperature. You should always read the instructions on your yeast and follow them to the letter. Here are some other ways to make the most of your yeast.

First, take yeast out of the fridge a few hours before you intend to use it. Allowing it to slowly reach room temperature prevents it from being shocked and not performing well.

Second, always use a thermometer, or a Fermometer. It's easy to cut corners by saying "this feels like it's the right temperature." But resting your hand on a carboy is not enough. Buy a few stick-on thermometers. You can find them listed as adhesive thermometers or Fermometers. They are a relatively inexpensive tool that will help you maintain the right temperature throughout your brewing. In addition to helping alert you to your desired fermentation temperature, they also let you monitor where you are storing your brews and can alert you to any temperature changes. The height of your ceilings, size of your space, and placement of in-home thermostats mean that what you see isn't necessarily what you get. A Fermometer gives you an exact reading of your brew's temperature exactly where it sits.

Light and Heat: Your Brew's Kryptonite

Want to destroy your home brew? Of course not! So be mindful of both heat and light, two deadly enemies.

Light

Have you ever noticed that most beer and wine bottles are brown or green? That's to protect the deliciousness inside from UV rays. It's like wearing sunglasses or sunscreen. That's right: the same harmful light rays that age your skin will destroy your brews. All stages of your brewing should be done out of direct sunlight to avoid light strike. Bottle in dark bottles, too, unless you plan on drinking your brew immediately.

In the wine world, the darker the bottle, the longer the wine should be aged. So a Châteauneuf-du-Pape in a nearly opaque bottle is meant to hang out for a while in your cellar, whereas a white wine in a clear bottle is meant for quick consumption. Apply this same rule when selecting the bottles to store your beer in, or always play it safe with dark bottles.

Heat

In addition to light, heat is bad for your brews. Tasters in the know will refer to the jimmy, nutty, sweet odor as "cooked." They may even throw around the word "madierized." If you never want to hear those words, be sure to store your homebrews at a cool temperature in the dark.

Measuring ABV

As a beginning home brewer, you likely won't measure ABV, or alcohol by volume. This percentage, found on every bottle of alcohol sold commercially, lets consumers know the punch the drink packs. In the case of home brewing, in the beginning the trick is getting down the process and developing a consistent recipe. But eventually you may get curious about the amount of alcohol. Also, if you decide to compete, you'll need to know the ABV for two reasons. First, most contests' rules require the ABV. Second, different types of alcohol must be in a specific range. Sack mead, for example, must have an ABV of at least fourteen percent. In your non-competitive brewing, measuring ABV helps you know when fermentation is complete. When you get the same reading several days apart you know it's done.

Measuring ABV isn't difficult if you've got the right tools, and if formulas in math don't send you running for the hills. You'll need to pick up a hydrometer, which should come with a test jar. You can grab a hydrometer at your local homebrew shop or online. To find your brew's ABV, follow these directions:

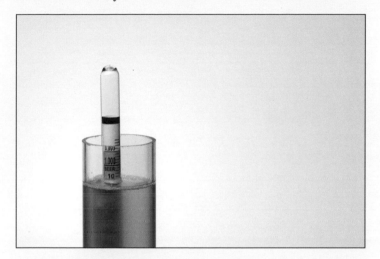

1. On a piece of paper write "OG:" and leave a space next to it to write. Under this write "FG:" and leave a space next to it to fill in. Underneath these write out the following formula:

$$(OG-FG) \times 131.25$$

1. Before pitching yeast, take a sample of your wort. Take enough to fill the hydrometer test tube most of the way. Better to have too much than too little.
2. Your hydrometer has one end that is heavier. I'm going to call this the "bottom." Slowly insert the bottom end of the hydrometer into the tube and release it gently, allowing it to float.
3. Look at where the liquid level is and write this reading down. It's usually not much over 1. Write this down where you left a space next to "OG:" This is your original gravity.

4. A few days into fermentation, remove another sample and take another reading. The number should decrease as fermentation progresses.

5. You'll take the final gravity (FG) reading prior to bottling. If you are going to carbonate your brew, you must take the reading prior to adding corn sugar to the wort.

6. Plug your original and final gravities into the formula to get the percentage of alcohol by volume in your final result.

For example:

> OG: 1.055
> FG: 1.01
> (1.055–1.01) x 131.25
> 0.045 x 131.25
> 5.90625% ABV

Once you get the number at the end, round it off neatly to the first decimal. In this case it becomes 5.9 percent ABV.

Some people do not like the above formula, which is a simplified version of the more traditional one. Let's run the same numbers in that formula and see what happens. There are a few things to remember when using this more complicated formula, especially if you don't regularly do math beyond simple arithmetic (e.g., balancing your checkbook). The Order of Operations is required, so we'll do things in parentheses first. When there are multiple types of arithmetic (multiplication and division), we'll multiply first. The Order of Operations is: parentheses, exponents, multiplication, division, addition, subtraction. In this case: parentheses, then multiplication, and finally division.

$$ABV = [76.08 \text{ x } (OG\text{-}FG) \text{ / } (1.775\text{-}OG)] \text{ x } (FG/0.794)$$

OG: 1.055

FG: 1.01

[76.08 x (1.055–1.01) / (1.775–1.055)] x (1.01/0.794)

[76.08 x 0.045 / 0.72] x (1.272040302)

[3.4236 / 0.72] x 1.272040302

4.755 x 1.272040302

6.048551637

6% ABV

The difference between the ABV found using the complicated formula and the simplified formula was about fourteen tenths. It's fine to use the simplified formula, especially when you're just brewing as a hobby. There are plenty of online calculators available, too, or you can make a simple Excel spreadsheet using easy formulas. Here's the one I use:

A1: Enter the text "OG"

A2: Enter the text "FG"

B1: Enter original gravity

B2: Enter final gravity

C1: carefully type the formula "=(B1-B2)*131.25"

If you want to use the full formula, you can also use a spreadsheet. Keep everything the same, except in C1 carefully type the formula "=(76.08*(B1-B2)/(1.775-B1))*(B2/0.794)"

Understanding Yeast

While it doesn't affect the flavor much, yeast is the most important ingredient in your meads, ciders, and herbal wines. Without yeast, your brews would be watered down, sweet concoctions. There wouldn't be alcohol or carbonation in your brews.

Yeast are single-celled fungi. They are tiny, egg-shaped organisms whose scientific name, *Saccharomyces Cerevisiae*, means "sugar eating fungus."[27] Could there be a better description? No! Yeast love sugar in several forms, which is especially exciting to home brewers. While you can use traditional white sugar, you can also use sucrose, fructose, glucose, or maltose. Maltose is specific to beer, though, and doesn't get used in the brewing this book will teach you.

Sucrose

Sucrose is table sugar, or what you think of when you think of sugar. It is found in all plants and usually extracted from beet

---

27 Red Star Yeast. "The Science of Yeast." *Redstaryeast.com/science-yeast/what-is-yeast/.* n.p. n.d. Web.

or cane. Sucrose consists of twelve carbon atoms, twenty-two hydrogen atoms, and eleven oxygen atoms. It is the most common form of sugar. Brown sugar is also sucrose, but late harvest with high amounts of molasses. It is fine to use in brewing, but can be difficult to store. Brown sugar hardens unless properly stored. Sucrose is sometimes refined using high temperatures achieved through the burning of bone char. These sugars are a no-no for vegans.

Fructose

Fructose is fruit sugar. It consists of six carbon atoms, twelve hydrogen atoms, and six oxygen atoms. It is often extracted from beets, cane, and maize. Fructose is what makes honey, maple syrup, molasses, tree and vine fruits, and berries sweet. It is also found in honey, flowers, and root vegetables. It is the reason sugar doesn't need to be added to mead and some fruit wines.

Glucose

Glucose is found in many of the same places as fructose and in many carbohydrates. The makeup of glucose is six carbon atoms, twelve hydrogen atoms, and six oxygen atoms. The most common glucose used in brewing is corn sugar, which is added to bottles to carbonate brews.

Home brewing, and all brewing, is the process of taking sugar, water, and ingredients that give the final product its flavor, and adding yeast to cause fermentation. Yeast is a living organism. When added to the other ingredients and kept at the right temperature, the yeast eats sugars. Its waste products are carbon dioxide and ethyl alcohol, giving your brews effervescence and alcoholic content.

The initial oxygen added to your must through aeration, prior to adding yeast, helps the yeast multiply. Once the oxygen is gone, fermentation can take place. Eventually its own waste, the alcohol, kills the yeast. This will end the fermentation process. The more sugar the yeast is able to metabolize, the higher the alcohol content of the final product.

The type of yeast used and the length of fermentation influence the amount of alcohol your brew ends up with and can affect the flavor of your final product. The recipes in this book include suggested yeasts. These were selected to help you reach and maintain proper fermentation easily.

There are a few things to keep in mind when experimenting with yeast.

If You're Brewing . . .	You Can't Go Wrong With . . .	Because . . .
Mead	Lalvin D-47	This white wine yeast ferments quickly and is a great starting yeast for making traditional mead.
Cider	Specialty Cider Yeast	It is bred and labeled as such because it works really well in cider. In the beginning, going with a yeast like this will help you get through the process. Eventually, feel free to experiment. If you cannot find cider yeast, champagne yeast is a favorite among home brewers making cider. It's hardy, easy to get fermenting, and often produces apple flavors and textures on the palate.
Herbal Wine	Montrachet	When starting out, this is an excellent yeast. It has a high alcohol tolerance, which means your fermentation is not likely to stall. It won't override tannins, making sure that your wines are not overly sweet.

These yeasts will make life easy for you at the beginning of your brewing journey, but there are things to keep in mind. First, always follow the directions that come on the yeast. Store them at the correct temperature and rehydrate according to the exact directions. A big part of this is making sure that you monitor the temperature of the yeast.

Take your yeast out of the fridge a few hours before pitching. Taking it from the fridge and adding it to warm water is a good way to shock the yeast, which can prevent fermentation. Don't shock your yeast. The temperature range is on the packet, so warm it up by taking it out and then add it to the water at the top end of the temperature. Always store your primary fermentation vessel in a room with a stable temperature within the range.

Vegan Home Brewing

Since high school I've crossed paths with several vegans, people who live according to guidelines established by six non-dairy vegetarians in 1944. I've always been interested in the lifestyle and philosophy, and when I blog about home brewing I always try to include notes for vegans because, as strange as it sounds, consumption of alcohol can be difficult for them.

What Is a Vegan?

These days there are people who eat a vegan diet but may not be vegan. Am I splitting hairs? Maybe. But it's an important distinction, especially when thinking about dietary choices.

If we look back at the five who started the movement in 1944 it's easy to see that veganism was about more than being non-dairy vegetarians. It was about a lifestyle. Leslie Cross suggested, in 1949, that a vegan lifestyle was "the emancipation of animals from exploitation by man." Later, this lifestyle was clarified. "To seek an end to the use of animals by man for food, commodities, work, hunting, vivisection and by all other uses involving exploitation of animal life by man."

The word vegan was created by taking the beginning and end of the word "vegetarian" and was meant to reflect "the beginning and end of vegetarian." The lifestyle means abstaining from any use of animals. Thus a strict vegan does not purchase leather furnishings, clothing, or accessories. He also doesn't use honey.

What's this have to do with home brewing?

Non-Vegan Ingredients

Several ingredients used in home brewing are not strictly vegan; none are necessary to the overall process, but they do serve a purpose. None of the cider or herbal wine recipes in this book call for animal-derived products, but if you grow in your brewing you might see these ingredients in other recipes. If you're brewing for someone who adheres to a vegan diet, they may be okay with some of these ingredients because animals are not killed to obtain them. A traditional vegan, however, will not wish to ingest these. Here are some of the ingredients you should be aware of, what they're made from, and how they're used.

| Albumin | Protein found in blood | Found in beer brewing, used to help with head retention |
| Carmine | Acid found in insects | Red dye (goes by several names) |

Casein	Protein found in cow's milk	Clarifies
Charcoal	Carbon ash residue, often from burned animal parts like bone	Filters
Diatomaceous earth	Ground earth often including fossils and seashells	Filters
Gelatin	Found in cattle or pig skin, connective tissue, and bones	Clarifies
Glyceryl Monostearate	Produced by the body when breaking down fats	Controls foam, emulsifier
Isinglass	Dried swim bladders	Clarifies
Lactose	Compound found in milk	Adds sweetness and body
Pepsin	Enzyme usually derived from pork	Emulsifier

The Sugar Question

Home brewing requires sugar for the yeast to work. Some white sugar is still made white using bone char because it reaches higher temperatures. These sugars are usually marked as "refined." You can likely find unrefined sugars in your local grocery store. You can also check with your local health food store to find out which sugars are safe for vegans.

Wait, What About Mead?

The question of mead is left to the consumer. Strict vegans will not drink it because bees make honey. Bees can be kept ethically and beekeeping helps the honeybee population but, by strict definition, mead is not okay for vegans.

Works Consulted/ Additional Resources

"Appalachian Regional Commission Overview." *State of New York*. Division of Local Government Services. Retrieved 2009-05-16.

Atlas Cider Co. "Hard Cider 101." *www.atlascider.com/hardciderhistory .html*. n.p. n.d. Web.

Cookthink. "Why do we bruise herbs?" *www.cookthink.com/reference /101/why_do_we_bruise Herbs?tag_id=503*" n.p. n.d. Web

Draft Magazine. "Tasting Terms." draftmag.com/tastingterms/. n.p. n.d.

Epicurious. "A Visual Guide to Fresh Herbs." *www.epicurious.com/ archive/seasonalcooking/Farmtotable/visualguidefreshherbs*. n.p. n.d.

Fine Cooking. "How to Bruise Herbs (On Purpose!)" *www.finecooking .com/article/how-to-bruise-herbs-on-purpose*. n.p. n.d. Web.

Glass with a Twist. "Mead Making Tips and Recipes." www.glass -withatwist.com/articles/Beer-And-Brewing/mead-tips-and -recipes. n.p. n.d. Web.

Kitchn. "The Science Behind Bruising Your Herbs." *www.thekitchn .com/the-science-behind-Bruising-yo-100988*. n.p. n.d. Web. 10 Nov. 2009.

Kitchn. "How to Check How Much Alcohol Is in Your Homebrew." *www.thekitchn.com/How-to-check-and-control-alcohol-levels-the- kitchns-beer-school-2015-217260*. n.p. n.d. 21 May 2015

Mother Earth Living. "How to Make Herbal Wine: Basic Worty Wine."*www .motherearthliving.com/cooking-methods/a-worty-wine-is-a-worthy -wine-basic*. n.p. n.d. Web. June/July 2005.

North Bay Brewery Tours. "Beginning Homebrewing: Measure Your ABV." *northbaybrewerytours.com/beginning-homebrewing-measure- your-abv/*. n.p. n.d. Web. 11 Feb. 2013.

Organic Authority. "Vegetable and Herb Stems: To Eat or Not to Eat." *www.organicauthority. Com/eco-chic-table/vegetable-herb-stems-cooking -stalks-eating-healthy.html*. n.p. n.d. Web. 5 Sep. 2011.

Pixie's Pocket. "One Gallon Mead and Wine Recipes." www.pixiespocket
.com/one-gallon-mead-recipes. n.p. n.d. Web.

Storm the Castle. "The Comprehensive Guide to Types of Mead."
*www.stormthecastle.com/mead/Articles/the-comprehensive-guide-to-
types-and-names-of-mead.htm.* n.p. n.d. Web.

The Herbal Academy. "How to Make Herbal Homemade Wine and Mead."
*www.theherbalacademy.com/herbal-homemade-wines-and-meads
/.* n.p. n.d. Web. 24 Feb. 2017.

Woodchuck Cider. "Cider History." *www.woodchuck.com/cider-101
/history.* n.p. n.d. Web.

Northern Brewer MagazineMead Made Easy website
Northwest Travel Magazine
Matching Food and Wine website
La Crema website
Baking Bites website
Wine Folly website
Pixie's Pocket website

Index

Brewing Notes

....

....

....

....

....

....

....

....

....

....

....

....

....

....

Brewing Notes

....

....

....

....

....

....

....

....

....

....

....

....

....

....

Brewing Notes

....

....

....

....

....

....

....

....

....

....

....

....

....

....

Brewing Notes

....

....

....

....

....

....

....

....

....

....

....

....

....

....

Brewing Notes

....

....

....

....

....

....

....

....

....

....

....

....

....

Brewing Notes

....

....

....

....

....

....

....

....

....

....

....

....

....

Brewing Notes

....

....

....

....

....

....

....

....

....

....

....

....

....

....

Brewing Notes

....

....

....

....

....

....

....

....

....

....

....

....

....

Brewing Notes

....

....

....

....

....

....

....

....

....

....

....

....

....

....

Brewing Notes

....

....

....

....

....

....

....

....

....

....

....

....

....

Brewing Notes

....

....

....

....

....

....

....

....

....

....

....

....

....

....

Brewing Notes

....

....

....

....

....

....

....

....

....

....

....

....

....

....

Brewing Notes

....

....

....

....

....

....

....

....

....

....

....

....

....

....

Brewing Notes

....

....

....

....

....

....

....

....

....

....

....

....

....

....